During the preparation of the manuscript for this book, Dr. Ernest R. Ranucci passed away. Dr. Ranucci was a most creative and talented teacher of mathematics. His speeches, workshops, and publications were an inspiration to thousands of teachers. The loss of Dr. Ranucci will be felt by all who knew him or his work.

# creating
# ESCHER-TYPE DRAWINGS

Margaret Macpherson
January 1986

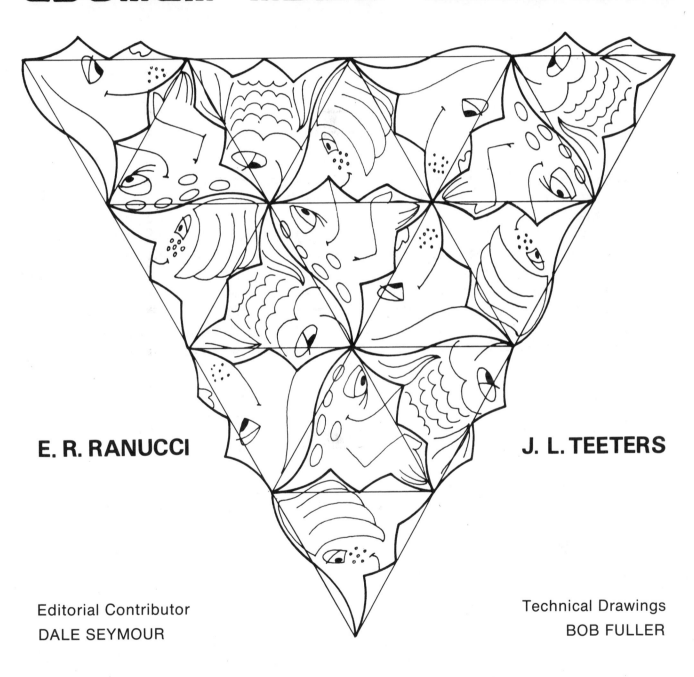

**E. R. RANUCCI**

**J. L. TEETERS**

Editorial Contributor
DALE SEYMOUR

Technical Drawings
BOB FULLER

CREATIVE PUBLICATIONS
PALO ALTO, CA 94303

**Limited Reproduction Permission:** The authors and publisher hereby grant permission to the teacher who purchases this book or the teacher for whom the book is purchased, to reproduce chapters 8 and 9 of this book for use with his or her students. Any further duplication is prohibited.

# ACKNOWLEDGMENTS

Lithographs by M. C. Escher on page 49 (untitled), page 81 ("Study of Regular Division of the Plane with Reptiles"), page 95 (untitled), page 123 ("Day and Night"), page 124 ("Study of Regular Division of the Plane with Birds"), page 127 ("Study of Regular Division of the Plane with Imaginary Animals"), page 129 ("Study of Regular Division of the Plane with Birds"), page 131 ("Cycle" and "Study of Regular Division of the Plane with Human Figures"), page 145 (untitled), page 191 ("Coast of Amalfi"), and page 193 ("Concave and Convex" and an untitled work) are reproduced by permission of the Escher Foundation, Haags Gemeentemuseum, The Hague. ©The Escher Foundation 1977. [Prints for reproduction of "Day and Night," "Cycle," and "Concave and Convex" furnished courtesy of Vorpal Galleries of New York, Chicago, San Francisco, and Laguna Beach.]

5 6 7 8 9 10 11 12 . 8 9 8 7 6 5 4

# TABLE OF CONTENTS

# INTRODUCTION

This book is written for those who are intrigued by the drawings of M.C. Escher, for those who seek to understand the mathematics underlying the drawings, and for those who would like to try their hand at creating their own imaginative patterns. It is not meant to be a complete treatise of the mathematics, crystallography, or color symmetry underlying Escher's tessellations of animate figures. Rather, it is a step-by-step explanation of the basic geometric ideas and drawing techniques which Escher seems to have employed in the creation of those tessellations.

As you read the explanations, allow some time to work on the drawing techniques. The worksheets in Chapter 8 will help you learn the techniques. Then let your imagination soar freely, and allow your inspiration to guide your drawings. Remember that Escher spent much of his lifetime perfecting his tessellations, so don't lose courage if your first attempts do not match the beauty and inventiveness of his work.

We have gained a great deal of enjoyment and satisfaction from our own studies of Escher-type tessellations, and hope that you will find our enthusiasm contagious.

Ernest R. Ranucci
Joseph L. Teeters

## PLANE TESSELLATIONS

*Plane tessellations* are the basis for Escher-type drawings presented in this book.
A plane tessellation is a complete covering of a plane by one or more figures in a repeating
pattern, with no overlapping of figures. (Hereafter in this book the word *tessellation* will
mean *plane tessellation.*)

Figure 1-1 shows some examples of tessellations.

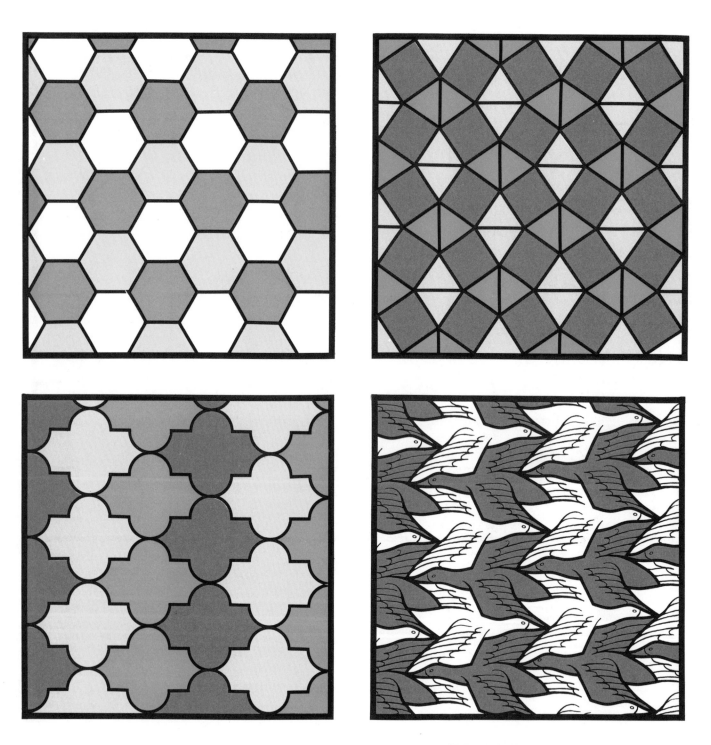

This drawing is based
on Escher's *Day and Night* woodcut
page 123

Figure 1-1

# TYPES OF TESSELLATIONS

## POLYGONAL TESSELLATIONS

A tessellation comprised entirely of polygons—such as triangles, quadrilaterals, hexagons—is a *polygonal tessellation.*

### Regular Tessellations

A polygon is a regular polygon if all of its sides have equal measures and all of its angles have equal measures. A tessellation is a *regular tessellation* if it is formed by congruent regular polygons. Only three regular polygons can form regular tessellations. These are: (1) an equilateral triangle, (2) a square, and (3) a regular hexagon. Examples are shown in Figure 1-2.

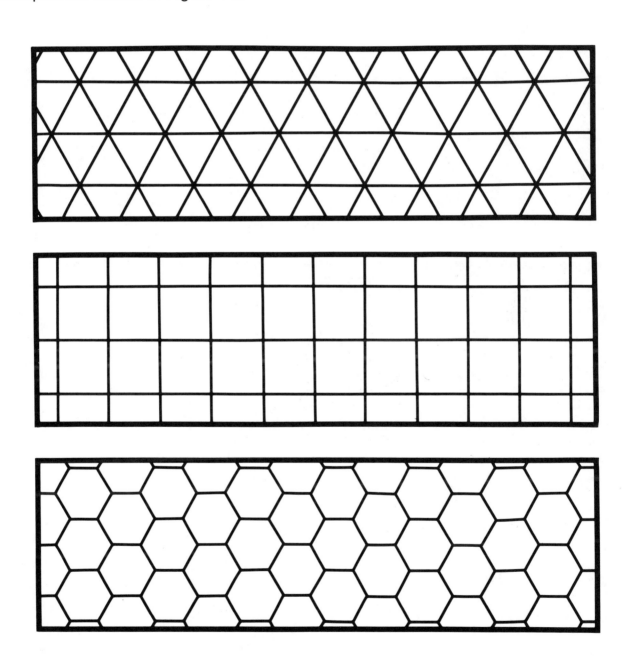

Figure 1-2

## Semiregular Tessellations

Combining two or more regular polygons to tessellate a plane results in a *semiregular tessellation* provided that the combination and order of the polygons that meet at a point *(vertex point)* are identical to the polygons that meet at any point of the tessellation.

Notice that the tessellations are named according to the number of sides and frequency of appearance at a vertex point. For example, the tessellation in Figure 1-3a is named 3.3.4.3.4 or $3^2.4.3.4$ because the configuration at any vertex point includes, in order, two 3-sided polygons, one 4-sided polygon, one 3-sided polygon, and one 4-sided polygon.

There are only eight semiregular tessellations. These are shown in Figure 1-3.

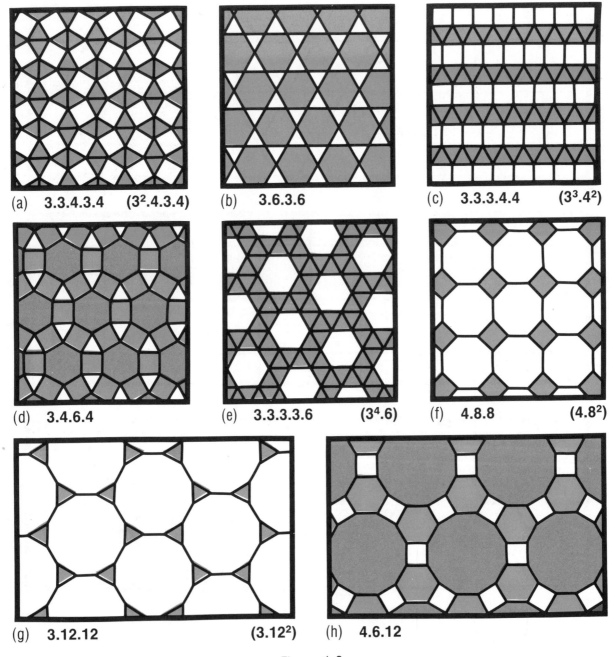

(a)  **3.3.4.3.4**  **($3^2$.4.3.4)**    (b)  **3.6.3.6**    (c)  **3.3.3.4.4**  **($3^3$.$4^2$)**

(d)  **3.4.6.4**    (e)  **3.3.3.3.6**  **($3^4$.6)**    (f)  **4.8.8**  **($4.8^2$)**

(g)  **3.12.12**  **($3.12^2$)**    (h)  **4.6.12**

Figure 1-3

**4**

## Nonregular Polygonal Tessellations

A number of polygonal shapes and combinations of shapes create tessellations. The following examples will provide some notion of the extensive possibilities.

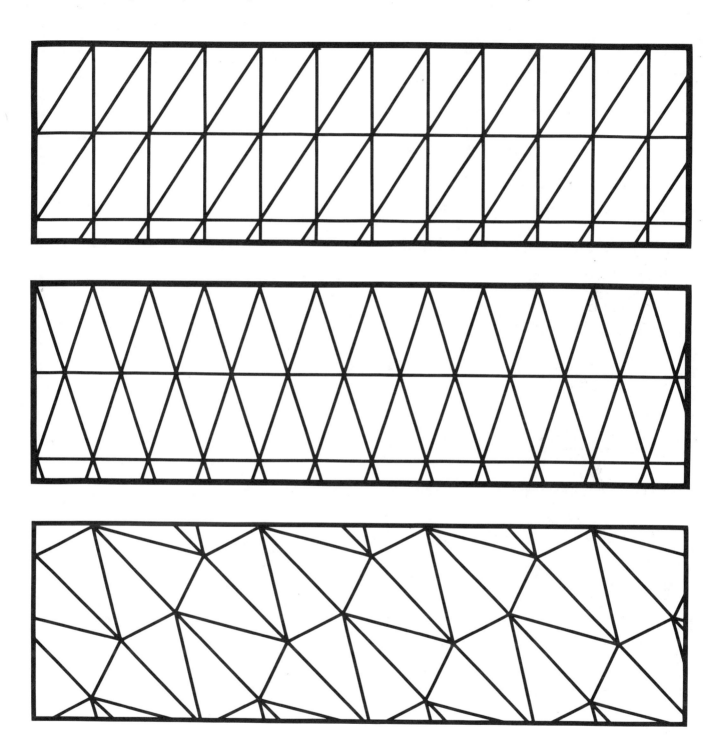

Figure 1-4
Tessellations of Triangles

Figure 1-5
Tessellations of Quadrilaterals

6

Figure 1-6
Tessellations of Pentagons

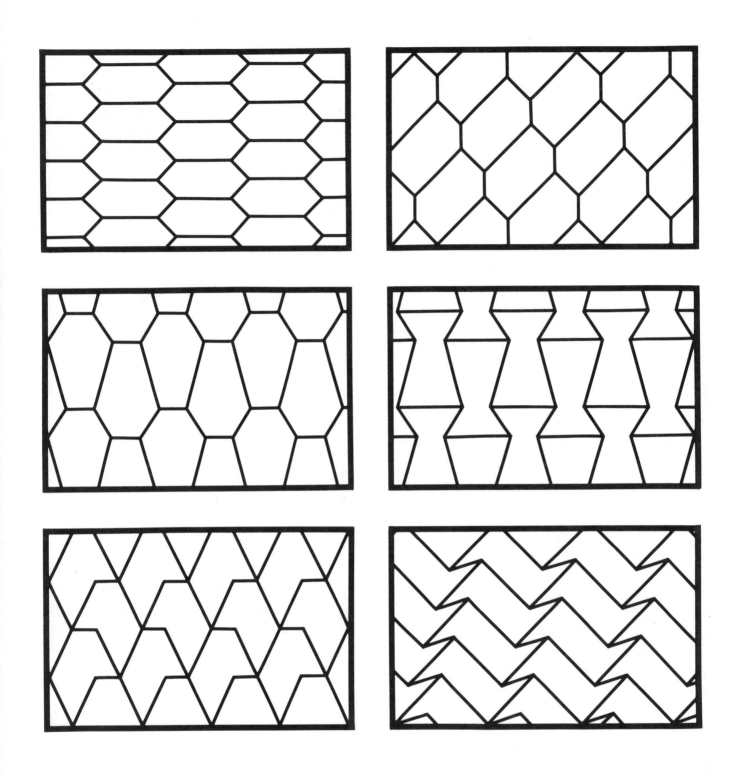

Figure 1-7
Tessellations of Hexagons

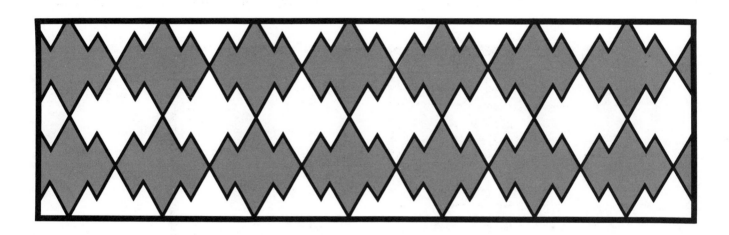

Figure 1-8
Tessellations Formed by
a Variety of Polygons

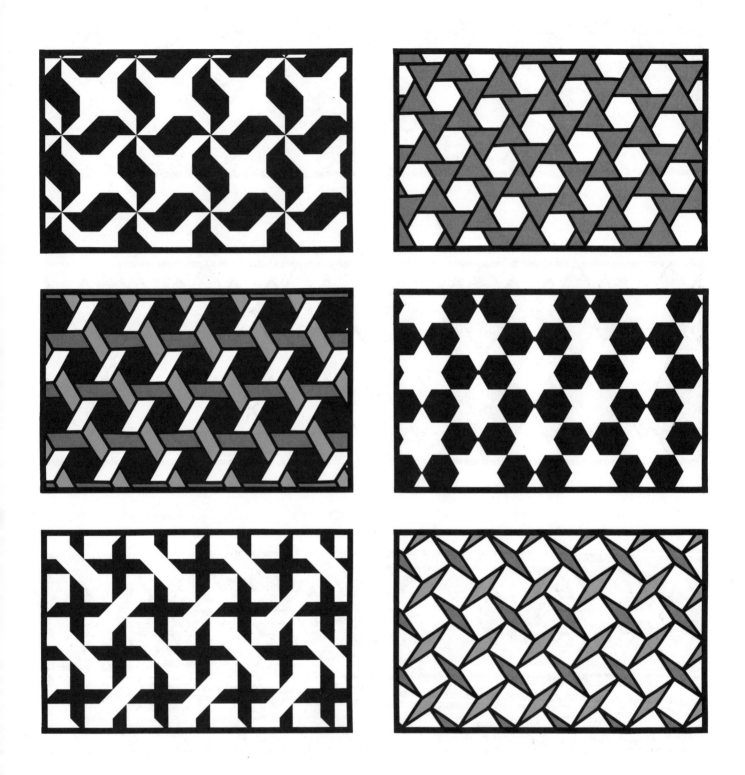

Figure 1-9
Tessellations Formed by
Combinations of Polygons

## NONPOLYGONAL TESSELLATIONS

Figure 1-10 shows some examples of tessellations formed by plane closed figures that are not all polygons.

Figure 1-10

# THE MATHEMATICS OF TESSELLATIONS

## FULL-TURN

The sum of the measures of all the angles about a point in a plane is equal to 360°. A *full-turn* is a complete rotation through 360°.

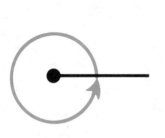

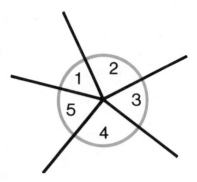

Full-turn
360°

The sum of the angles is 360°.

$$m\angle 1 + m\angle 2 + m\angle 3 + m\angle 4 + m\angle 5 = 360°$$

Figure 1-11

## HALF-TURN

The sum of the measures of all the angles on one side of a straight line is 180°. A *half-turn* is a rotation through 180°.

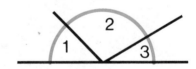

Half-turn
180°

The sum of the angles is 180°.

$$m\angle 1 + m\angle 2 + m\angle 3 = 180°$$

Figure 1-12

12

# INTERIOR ANGLE MEASURE OF POLYGONS

## Measure of the Interior Angles of a Triangle

*The sum of the measures of the interior angles of any triangle is 180°.* This can be demonstrated as follows:

Think of cutting off the corners of a triangle (Figure 1-13a) and placing them about a given point (Figure 1-13b). The sum of the measures of the angles on one side of a line is 180°. This can also be demonstrated by turning a pencil through the three angles of a triangle, thereby rotating the pencil through a half-turn or 180° (Figure 1-13c–i).

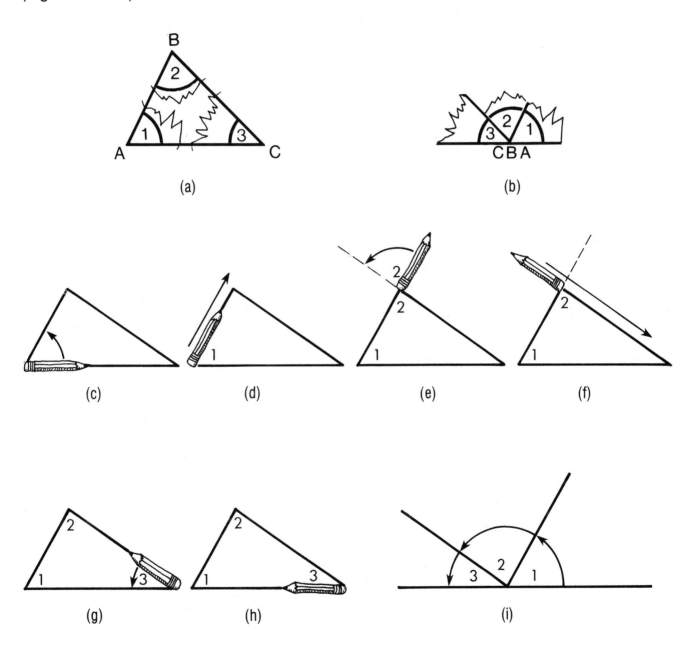

Figure 1-13

## Measure of the Interior Angles of a Quadrilateral

Any quadrilateral can be divided into two triangular regions by a diagonal. The sum of the measures of the angles of each triangle is 180°; therefore, *the sum of the measures of the interior angles of any quadrilateral is 360°*.

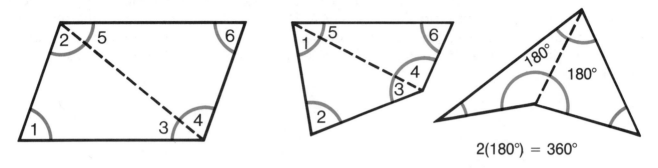

2(180°) = 360°

Figure 1-14
Quadrilaterals
m∠1 + m∠2 + m∠3 + m∠4 + m∠5 + m∠6 = 360°

## Measure of the Interior Angles of Any Polygon

Every polygon can be divided into triangular regions by drawing selected diagonals.

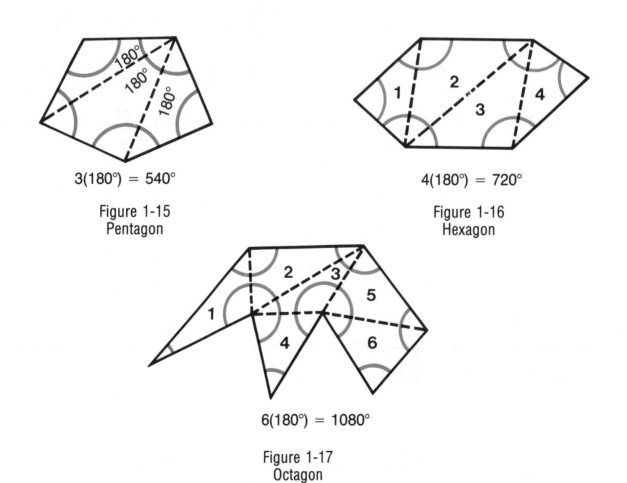

3(180°) = 540°

Figure 1-15
Pentagon

4(180°) = 720°

Figure 1-16
Hexagon

6(180°) = 1080°

Figure 1-17
Octagon

A polygon with five sides can be divided into three triangular regions, six sides into four regions, seven sides into five regions, and so on. A polygon with *n* sides can be divided into (*n*−2) regions. *The sum of the measures of the interior angles of any n-sided polygon is (n−2)180 degrees. The measure of each of the angles of a regular n-sided polygon is* $\frac{(n-2)180}{n}$ *degrees.*

## ANGLE MEASURE IN POLYGONS

| Regular Polygon | Number of Sides/ Angles | Total Angle Measure | Measure of Each Interior Angle |
|---|---|---|---|
| triangle | 3 | 180° | 60° |
| quadrilateral | 4 | 360° | 90° |
| pentagon | 5 | 540° | 108° |
| hexagon | 6 | 720° | 120° |
| heptagon | 7 | 900° | $128\frac{4}{7}°$ |
| octagon | 8 | 1080° | 135° |
| · · · | · · · | · · · | · · · |
| n-gon | n | (n−2)180° | $\frac{(n-2)180°}{n}$ |

## POLYGONS THAT TESSELLATE

### Regular Polygons

There are only three *regular* polygons that can tessellate a plane without being combined with other polygons. They are (1) equilateral triangles, (2) squares, and (3) regular hexagons. The following illustrations show this to be true.

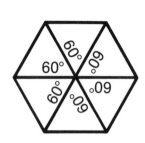

**Figure 1-18**
Equilateral Triangles
$6 \times 60° = 360°$

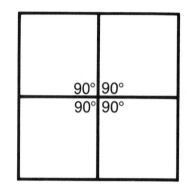

**Figure 1-19**
Squares
$4 \times 90° = 360°$

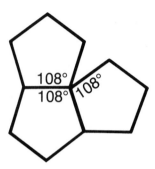

Does not tessellate

**Figure 1-20**
Pentagons
$3 \times 108° < 360°$
$4 \times 108° > 360°$

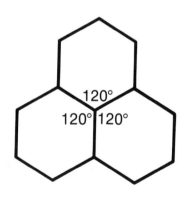

**Figure 1-21**
Hexagons
$3 \times 120° = 360°$

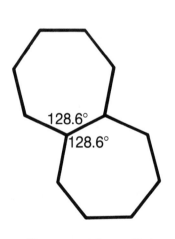

Does not tessellate

**Figure 1-22**
Heptagons
$2 \times 128+° < 360°$
$3 \times 128+° > 360°$

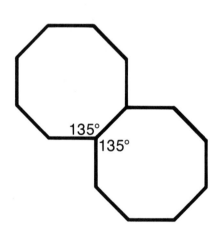

Does not tessellate

**Figure 1-23**
Octagons
$2 \times 135° < 360°$
$3 \times 135° > 360°$

## Triangles

*Any triangle will tessellate.* This is true because the sum of the measures of the angles of any triangle equals 180°. The examples in Figures 1-24 and 1-25 show how the three angles can be positioned to form a half-turn. Two types of repetitions form the tessellation, a parallelogram or a kite.

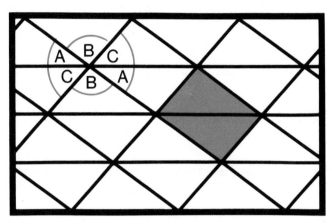

Parallelogram formed

Kite formed

Figure 1-24

$$2 (m\angle A + m\angle B + m\angle C) = 360°$$

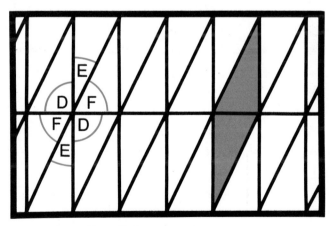

Parallelogram formed

Kite formed

Figure 1-25

$$2(m\angle D + m\angle E + m\angle F) = 360°$$

## Quadrilaterals

*Any quadrilateral will tessellate.* This is true because the sum of the measures of the angles of any quadrilateral equals 360°. See the examples in Figure 1-26.

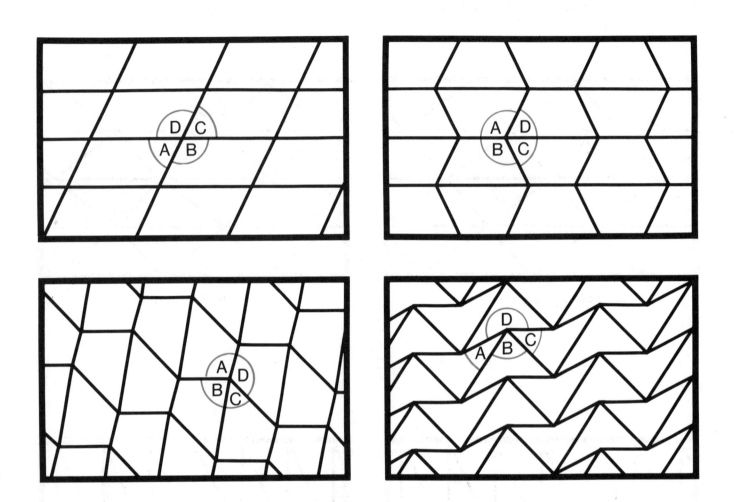

Figure 1-26

$$m\angle A + m\angle B + m\angle C + m\angle D = 360°$$

Tessellating triangles, quadrilaterals, and hexagons will constitute the basic underlying design patterns for most drawings in this book.

## SUMMARY

Only three *regular* polygons tessellate by themselves. These are: (1) an equilateral triangle, (2) a square, and (3) a regular hexagon. Certain polygons or combinations of polygons will tessellate under special conditions.

*Any* triangle or quadrilateral will tessellate the plane.

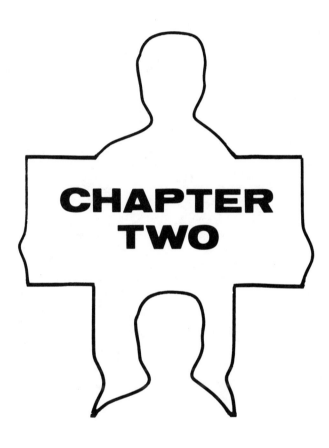

CHAPTER TWO

# TRANSFORMATIONS AND SYMMETRY

Transformations are used to form tessellations. A transformation is a correspondence or matching between points of the plane. We will consider three transformations: (1) translations or slides, (2) rotations or turns, and (3) reflections or flips.

## TRANSLATIONS

The operation of translating a figure in a plane involves a linear shift or slide of the figure in that plane. In Figure 2-1, quadrilateral ABCD has been translated to a new position in the plane (A'B'C'D'). Notice that $\overline{AA'}$, $\overline{BB'}$, $\overline{CC'}$, and $\overline{DD'}$ are all parallel.

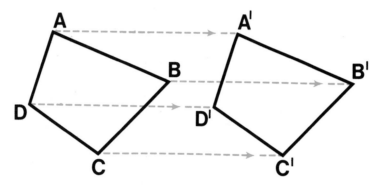

Figure 2-1

It is often easier to think of a translation as a *slide*. The transformation shown in Figure 2-2 is *not a translation* because it is *not linear*. Rotation of the figure has taken place; that is, $\overline{DD'}$, $\overline{EE'}$, $\overline{FF'}$, and $\overline{GG'}$ are not parallel.

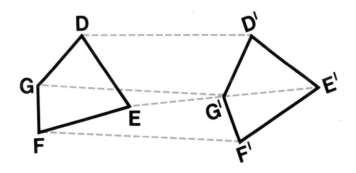

Figure 2-2
Not a Translation

The properties of size, shape, and orientation remain invariant (unchanged) under the operation of translation.

# ROTATIONS

The operation of rotation of a figure in a plane involves turning the figure about a given point in the plane, called the *center of rotation.* Each point in the figure is mapped on the arc of concentric circles having as a center the center of rotation. In Figure 2-3, triangle ABC has been rotated to a new position in the plane (triangle A B'C'). Notice that point A is the center of rotation.

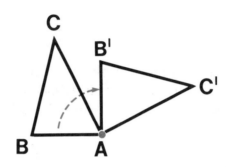

Figure 2-3

The center of rotation may or may not be a point in the figure itself.

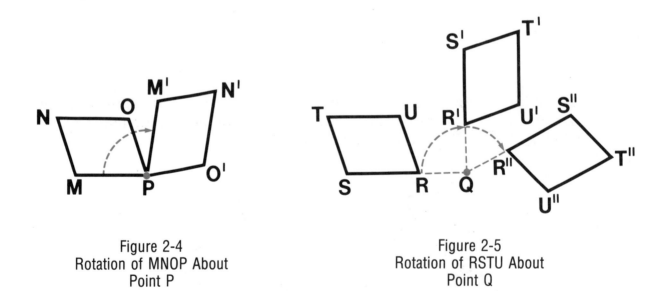

Figure 2-4
Rotation of MNOP About
Point P

Figure 2-5
Rotation of RSTU About
Point Q

The properties of size and shape remain invariant under the operation of rotation.

## REFLECTIONS

A reflection is a flipping of points of the plane about a line, called the *line of reflection* or the *mirror.* In Figure 2-6, the figure is reflected through line $\ell$. P′ is the reflected image of P, and P is the reflected image of P .

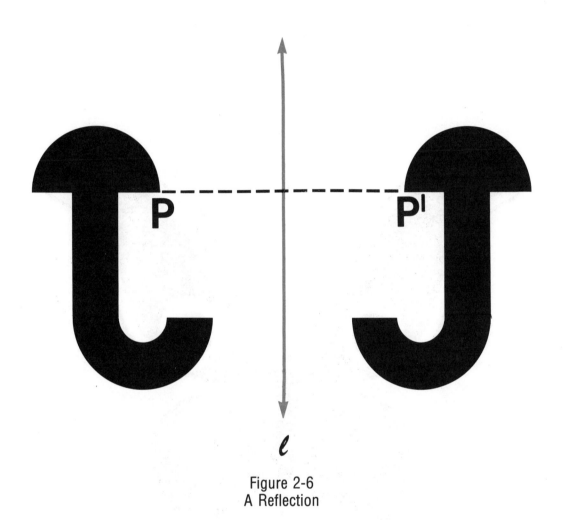

Figure 2-6
A Reflection

The properties of size and shape remain invariant under the operation of reflection. Notice in Figure 2-6 that the figure which has been reflected can not be translated or rotated to coincide with its reflection.

It is often simpler to think of a translation as a *slide,* a rotation as a *turn,* and a reflection as a *flip.*

# PLANE SYMMETRY

## LINE SYMMETRY

A figure has line symmetry if there is a line of reflection such that each point in the figure can be reflected into the figure.

In Figure 2-7, the drawing is symmetric with respect to the line of symmetry, $\ell$.

Figure 2-7
Figure Having Line Symmetry

Line symmetry has many synonyms. Line symmetry is sometimes referred to as *mirror symmetry*, or *axial symmetry*, or *bilateral symmetry*, or *reflective symmetry*. The line of symmetry is likewise referred to in many ways, some of which are: *axis of symmetry, mirror line, mirror*, and *line of reflection*.

Shown in Figure 2-8 are several geometric figures that have line symmetry. The line of symmetry is shown in red.

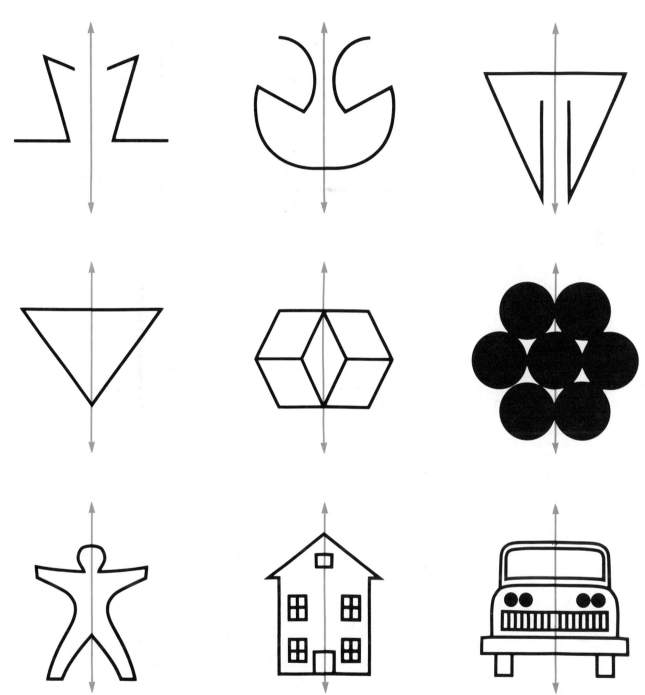

Figure 2-8
Figures Having Line Symmetry

A good test to see if a plane figure has line symmetry is to fold the paper along the assumed line of symmetry. If each point of the figure on one side of the fold coincides with a corresponding point on the other side, the figure is symmetric with respect to the fold line.

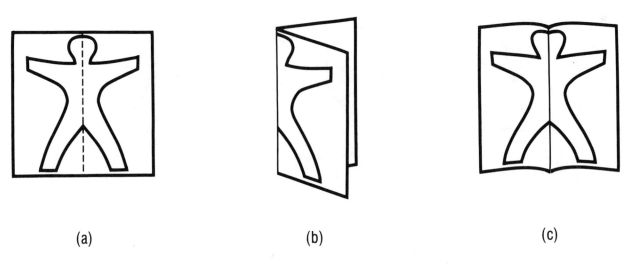

(a)                    (b)                    (c)

Figure 2-9

Another way to test a figure for symmetry is to place a mirror along the assumed line of symmetry (Figure 2-10). If the figure and its reflection are identical to the original figure, the figure is symmetric with respect to the "mirror line."

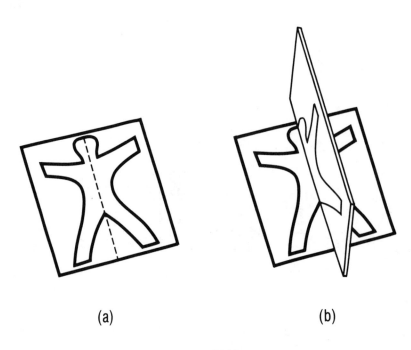

(a)                    (b)

Figure 2-10

A figure may have more than one line of symmetry. An equilateral triangle has three lines of symmetry.

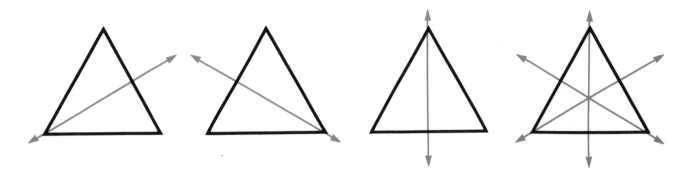

Figure 2-11

A square has four lines of symmetry.

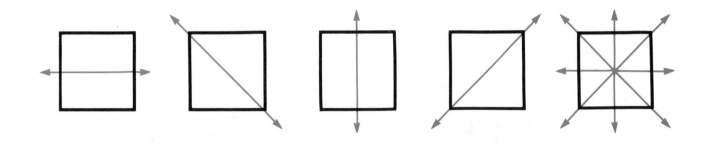

Figure 2-12

A regular *n*-sided polygon has *n* lines of symmetry.

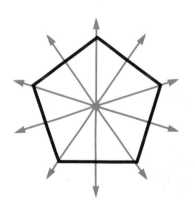
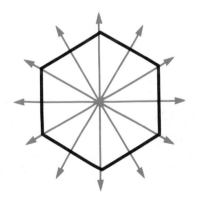

Figure 2-13
Regular Pentagon
(five lines of symmetry)

Figure 2-14
Regular Hexagon
(six lines of symmetry)

Figure 2-15
Regular Octagon
(eight lines of symmetry)

27

Any line through the center of a circle is a line of symmetry. The circle is the most symmetric of all plane figures

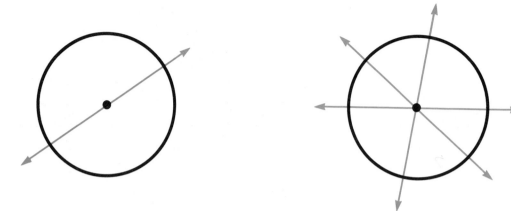

Figure 2-16

Many designs, trademarks, and logos are created to have one or more lines of symmetry. Some examples are shown in Figure 2-17.

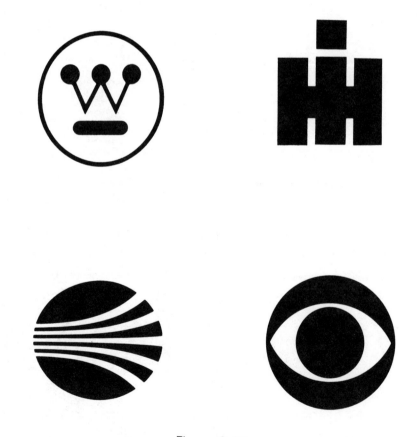

Figure 2-17

Notice which letters of the alphabet have vertical symmetry (Figure 2-18).

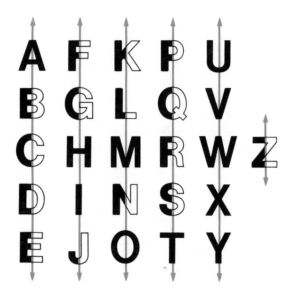

Figure 2-18

Notice which letters of the alphabet have horizontal symmetry (Figure 2-19).

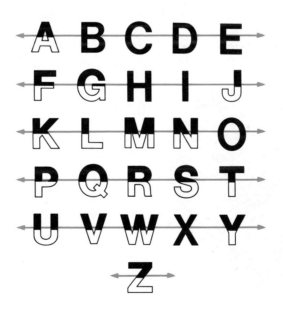

Figure 2-19

POINT SYMMETRY

A figure has point symmetry if a half-turn makes the figure coincide with itself. The center point is called the *point of symmetry.* In Figure 2-20, P is the point of symmetry; $\overline{AP} \cong \overline{A'P}$ and $\overline{BP} \cong \overline{B'P}$.

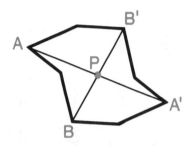

Figure 2-20
Figure Having Point Symmetry

Point symmetry is sometimes called *radial symmetry.* A simple test to see if a figure has point symmetry is to turn the figure 180°. If it is identical to the figure in its original position, it has point symmetry. Shown in Figure 2-21 are several geometric figures that have point symmetry. The point of symmetry is shown in red.

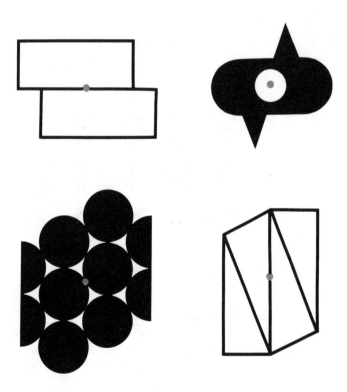

Figure 2-21
Figures Having Point Symmetry

30

Two figures have point symmetry if one is a 180° rotation of the other about a point of symmetry.

A figure may have both line symmetry and point symmetry. Examples of such figures are shown in Figure 2-22.

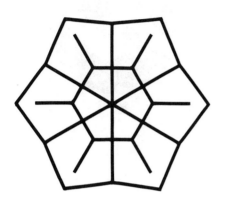  

Figure 2-22

Shown in Figure 2-23 are figures which have line symmetry but no point symmetry.

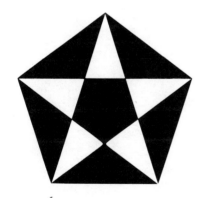  

Figure 2-23

Shown in Figure 2-24 are figures which have point symmetry but no line symmetry.

Figure 2-24

## ROTATIONAL SYMMETRY

Point symmetry is a special case of rotational symmetry. A figure has rotational symmetry if it can be rotated through less than 360° about a point to coincide with itself. An example of a figure that has rotational symmetry but which is not point symmetric is an equilateral triangle.

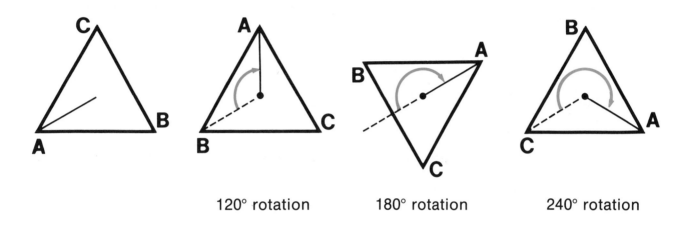

120° rotation          180° rotation          240° rotation

Figure 2-25

As you can see, rotations of 120° and 240° place the triangle in its original position; thus, the figure has rotational symmetry. A figure has point symmetry if it has a rotational symmetry of 180°. The figures below have rotational symmetry but no point symmetry.

Figure 2-26

A figure has $n$-fold symmetry if it coincides with itself when rotated through an angle of $\frac{360°}{n}$ about its point of symmetry. A square has fourfold symmetry. This is illustrated in Figure 2-27.

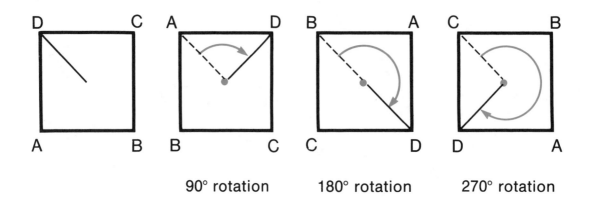

90° rotation    180° rotation    270° rotation

Figure 2-27
Example of Fourfold Symmetry

Shown in Figures 2-28 through 2-32 are various examples of rotational symmetry.

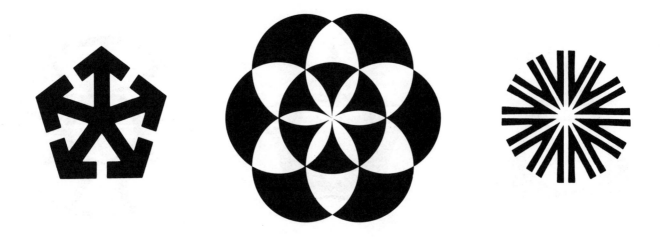

Figure 2-28
Figures Having Rotational Symmetry

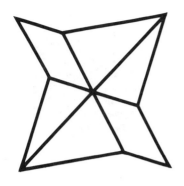  

Figure 2-29
Figures Having Twofold Rotational Symmetry

Figure 2-30
Figures Having Threefold Rotational Symmetry

  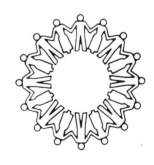

Figure 2-31
Figures Having Fourfold Rotational Symmetry

Figure 2-32
Figures Having Sixfold Rotational Symmetry

## SUMMARY

In *CREATING ESCHER-TYPE DRAWINGS,* we will be primarily interested in three transformations: (1) translations (slides), (2) rotations (turns), and (3) reflections (flips). Two kinds of symmetries that will be important in our work are: (1) reflective symmetry (line symmetry), and (2) rotational symmetry. Line symmetry involves reflections about a line. Point symmetry, which is a special case of rotational symmetry, involves half-turns about a point.

(See worksheets 8-1 through 8-6.)

CHAPTER
THREE

# ALTERING BY TRANSLATION

Many of Escher's drawings can be thought of as alterations of tessellating polygons. This chapter will deal with drawings formed by altering the sides of polygons and then *translating* them. As you recall from the previous chapter, a translation is a slide along a line.

## ALTERING PARALLELOGRAMS BY TRANSLATION

One regular tessellation is formed by congruent squares. Let's begin this investigation by altering the basic tessellating square.

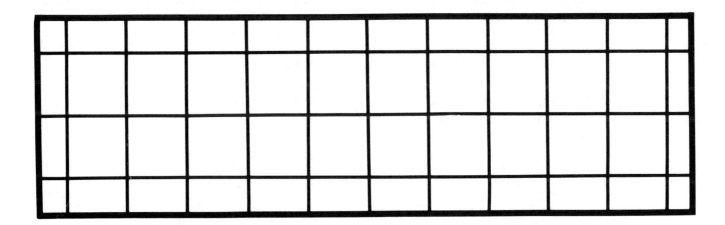

Figure 3-1

We make an alteration on one side of a square, as shown in Figure 3-2. If this altered line is translated to the opposite side of the square, we have a new shape that tessellates. Notice that the area of the original square remains invariant; that is, the area of the new shape is equal to the area of the original square.

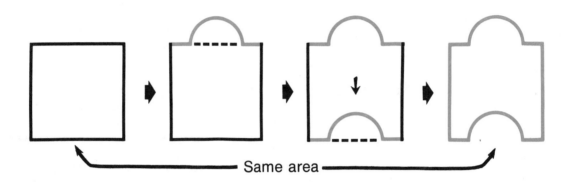

Same area

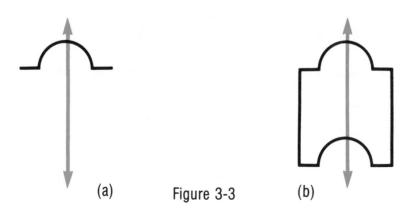

Figure 3-2
Translating an Altered Side of a Square

In Figure 3-2, the altered shape has line symmetry (Figure 3-3a). The altered sides of the square have the same line of symmetry (Figure 3-3b).

(a)          Figure 3-3          (b)

**40**

When altering a square by translating opposite sides to form a new tessellating figure, the alteration *does not* have to be symmetrical. The alteration of the square in Figure 3-4 serves as an example.

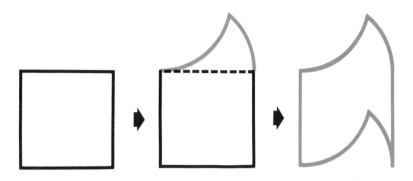

Figure 3-4
Nonsymmetrical Alteration of a Square

In the two previous examples, the alterations were made on only one side of the line being altered. This is not a requirement, however, for forming a tessellating shape. The example in Figure 3-5 shows a square whose sides have been altered both above and below the original side.

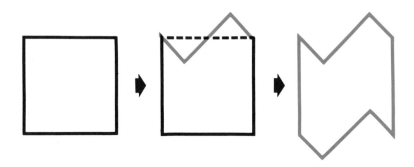

Figure 3-5
Alteration Above and Below
the Original Line

To make sure that opposite altered sides are identical, it may be helpful to trace one of the lines or the entire figure. First, modify one side of the polygon (Figure 3-6b). Place a piece of tracing paper over the new curve and trace it (Figure 3-6c). Then move the traced curve so that the endpoints coincide (Figure 3-6e), and trace or use a piece of carbon paper to transfer the identical curve in its position (Figure 3-6f).

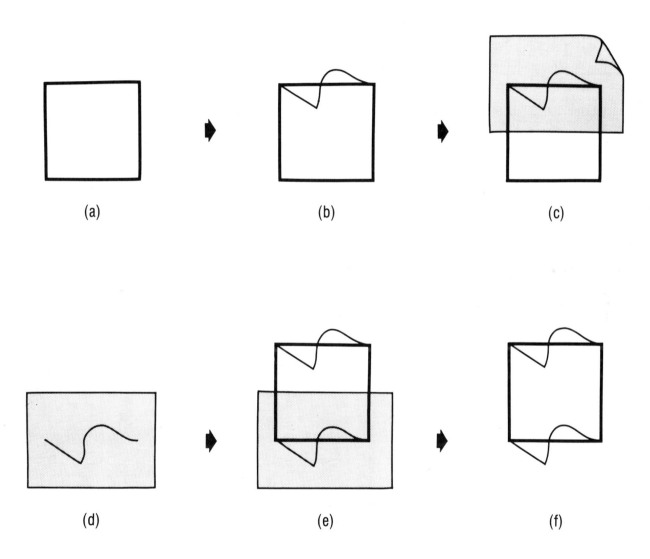

Figure 3-6

Two specific silhouettes or illustrations of animate figures are shown in Figure 3-7. They are examples of alterations of opposite sides of a rectangular grid by translation.

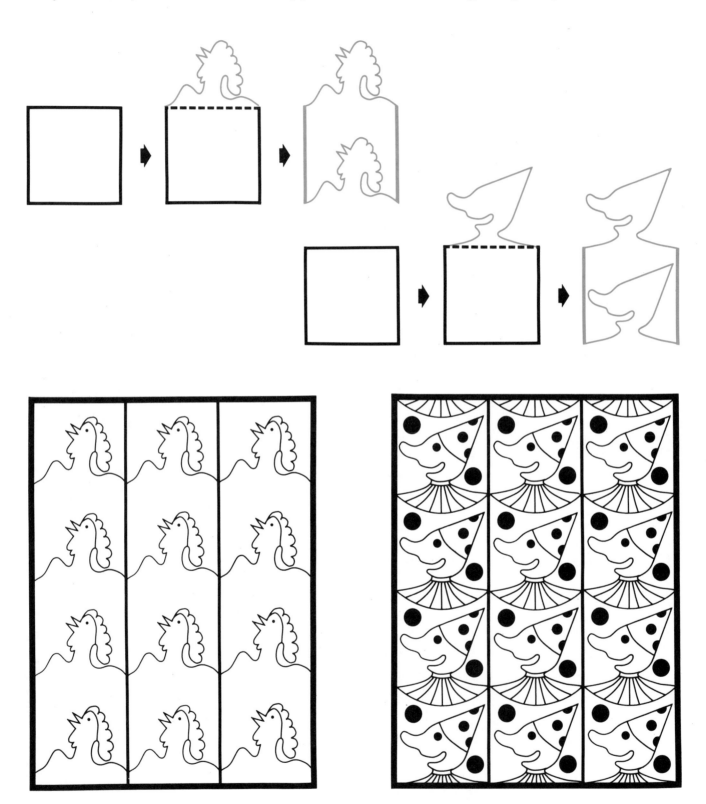

Figure 3-7

This technique of altering opposite sides of a rectangular tessellation can be applied to any parallelogram. The alteration in Figure 3-8 is somewhat more complex.

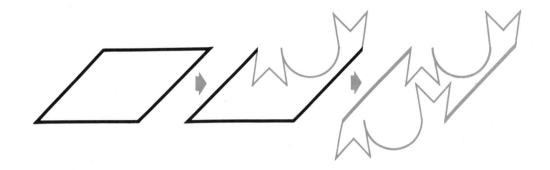

Figure 3-8
Altered Parallelograms

The examples thus far have illustrated the alteration of *one pair* of parallel, congruent opposite sides of a parallelogram. Tessellating shapes can be formed by applying this translation technique to *both* pairs of parallel sides. An example is shown in Figure 3-9.

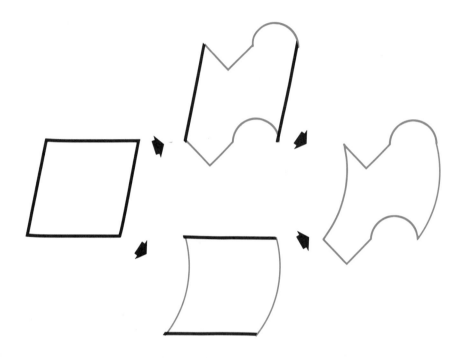

Figure 3-9
Altering Both Pairs of
Opposite Sides

Apply a dash of imagination and a flock of birds appears.

Figure 3-10

Shown below are more simple examples of tesselations of animate figures based on transformation of parallelograms through translations.

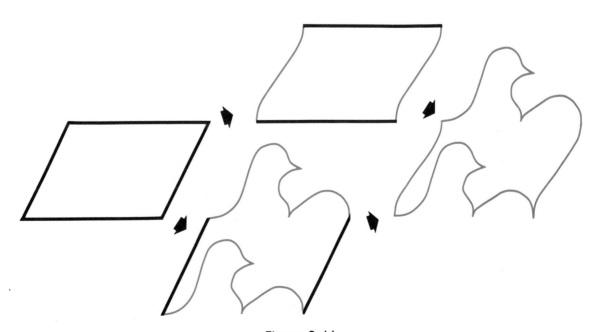

Figure 3-11

Figure 3-11 (continued)

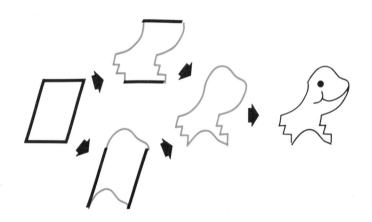

Figure 3-12

48

Shown in Figure 3-13a is one of Escher's designs that was based on translations within parallelograms:

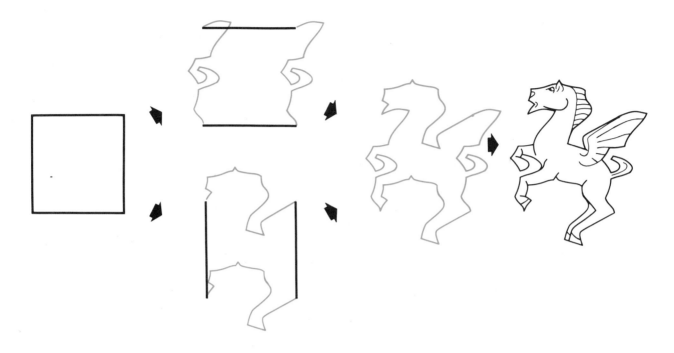

Figure 3-13 (a)

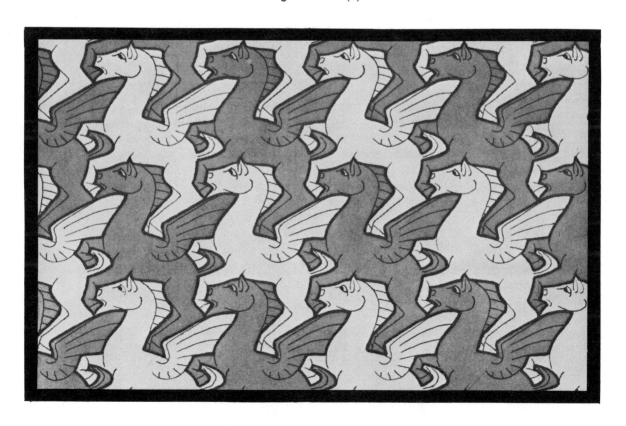

M. C. Escher. Untitled Work

Figure 3-13 (b)

There are two approaches to altering tessellating polygons into animate figures. One approach is to have some specific object in mind and to alter the lines to make the shape look like the object. This approach may require a bit of trial and error.

A second approach is to create a new shape and then use your imagination to see what you think it "looks like." The tessellation shown in Figure 3-14 is a modification of squares. Two "bumps" were used on the vertical sides and one "bump" on the horizontal side.

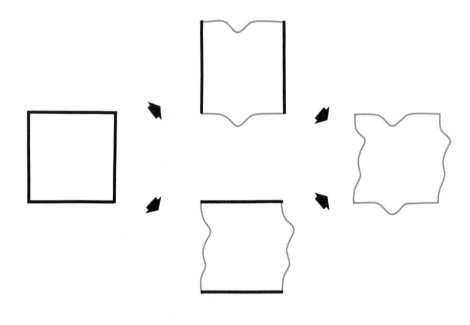

Figure 3-14

Does the new shape look like anything special to you? Does it remind you of anything? There are many things it could be.

It could be the head of a person wearing a feather in his cap.

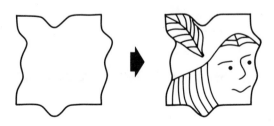

Figure 3-15

50

Figure 3-15 (continued)

If the basic shape is rotated 180°, it could be a pair of wrestlers.

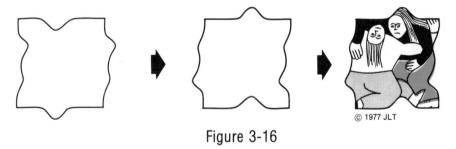

Figure 3-16

Here is a different altered square. What does it look like to you? Maybe a flying owl?

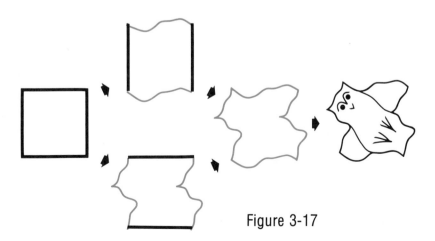

Figure 3-17

**51**

Figure 3-17 (continued)

Here is another example.

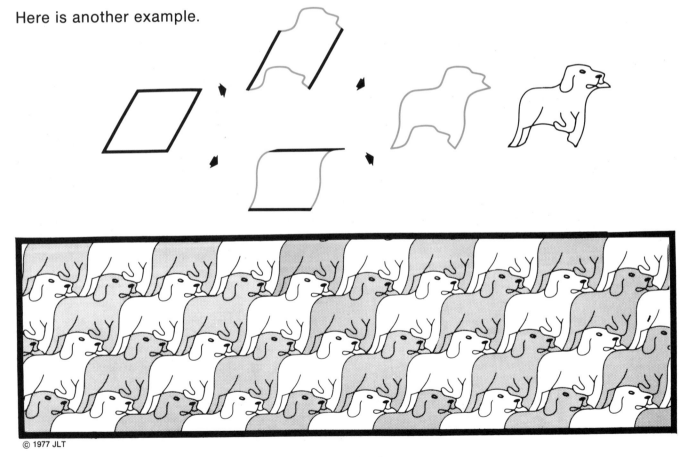

Figure 3-18

52

Even simple curves may remind you of something like a space ship.

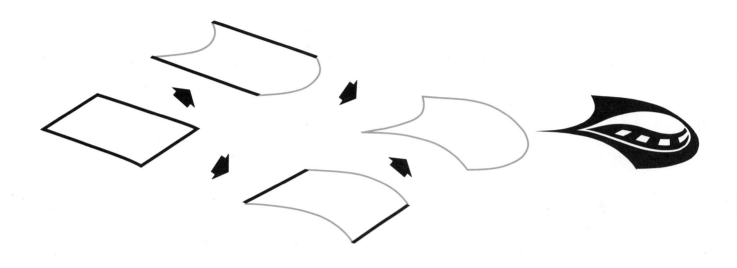

Figure 3-19

## ALTERING HEXAGONS BY TRANSLATION

We have seen that parallelograms can be altered to tessellate. Opposite sides of parallelograms are congruent and parallel. Now let's investigate another polygon whose opposite sides are parallel and congruent, the regular hexagon. We know from our study of Chapter 1 that regular hexagons tessellate.

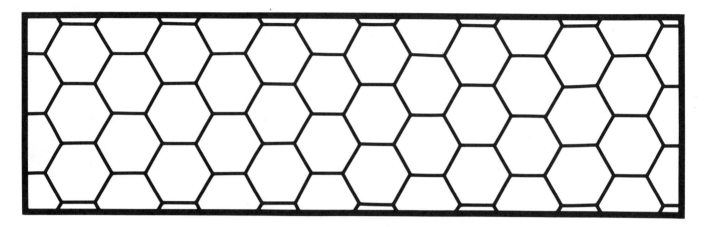

Figure 3-20

In the experiment shown in Figure 3-21, translating the alteration of opposite sides of a regular hexagon provides a new shape which tessellates. This technique can be applied to any regular hexagon to produce a tessellating shape.

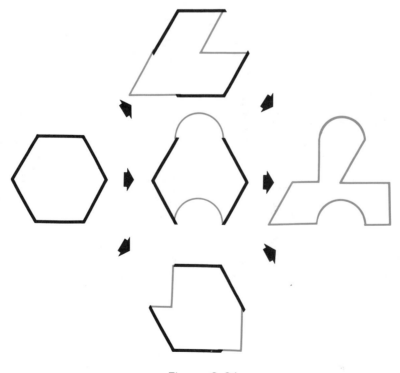

Figure 3-21

Figure 3-21 (continued)

The example in Figure 3-22 shows an animate figure.

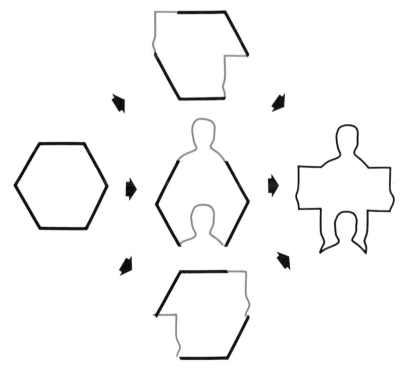

Figure 3-22

The regular hexagon and the final altered figure each have the same area. Each time a side of the hexagon was altered to increase the area of the closed figure, the opposite side was altered identically to reduce the area by the same amount.

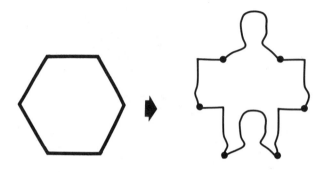

These two figures have identical areas.

Figure 3-23

In a regular hexagon, the opposite sides are congruent and parallel, and all six sides are congruent. In the hexagon shown in Figure 3-24, the opposite sides are congruent and parallel, but all six sides are not of the same length.

$\overline{AB} \cong \overline{ED}, \overline{AB} \parallel \overline{ED}$
$\overline{AF} \cong \overline{CD}, \overline{AF} \parallel \overline{CD}$
$\overline{FE} \cong \overline{BC}, \overline{FE} \parallel \overline{BC}$

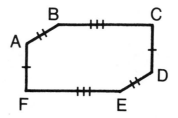

Figure 3-24

Let's try altering a hexagon by translating congruent, parallel opposite sides.

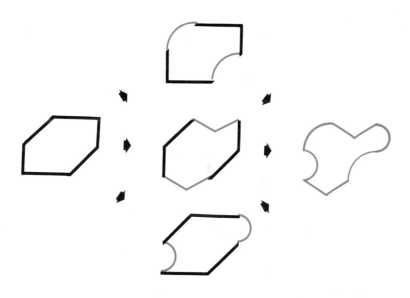

Figure 3-25

57

Figure 3-25 (continued)

The hexagonal region with parallel and congruent opposite sides can be separated into three parallelograms. These parallelograms can serve as the basic boundaries for tessellating patterns. Since the parallelograms provide a natural perspective, the total figure within the hexagon might appear three-dimensional.

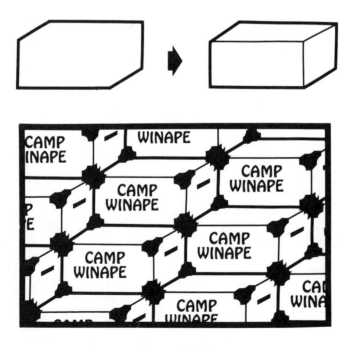

Figure 3-26

Figure 3-27 illustrates hexagonal regions divided into parallelograms.

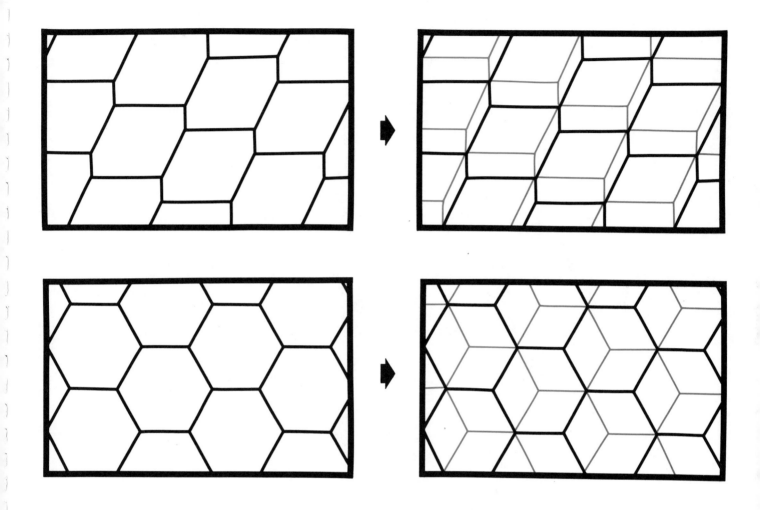

Figure 3-27

## SUMMARY

In this chapter, we have seen that tessellating parallelograms and hexagons having parallel and congruent opposite sides can be transformed into new shapes that will tessellate. These new shapes are created by translating the alteration of one side of the polygon to its opposite side. (See worksheets 8-7 through 8-8.)

# CHAPTER FOUR

# ALTERING BY ROTATION

## ALTERING POLYGONS BY ROTATION OF SIDES

### ALTERING TWO SIDES OF A TRIANGLE BY ROTATION

In Chapter 3 we discovered that curved-line tessellations could be formed by altering the parallel and congruent opposite sides of quadrilaterals and hexagons. Since triangles can not have opposite parallel sides, obviously the sides can not be altered by translation. Rotation, however, is another matter. We can alter a side of a triangle and rotate the alteration to either one of the adjacent sides. Notice in the example shown in Figure 4-1 that the point of rotation is an endpoint of the side.

Start with a triangle.

Change a side.

Rotate the changed side.

Use this figure to form a tessellation.

Figure 4-1

**63**

In the previous example the alteration happened to be symmetric about the midpoint of the side. The example in Figure 4-2 shows us that nonsymmetric alterations also create shapes that tessellate by themselves.

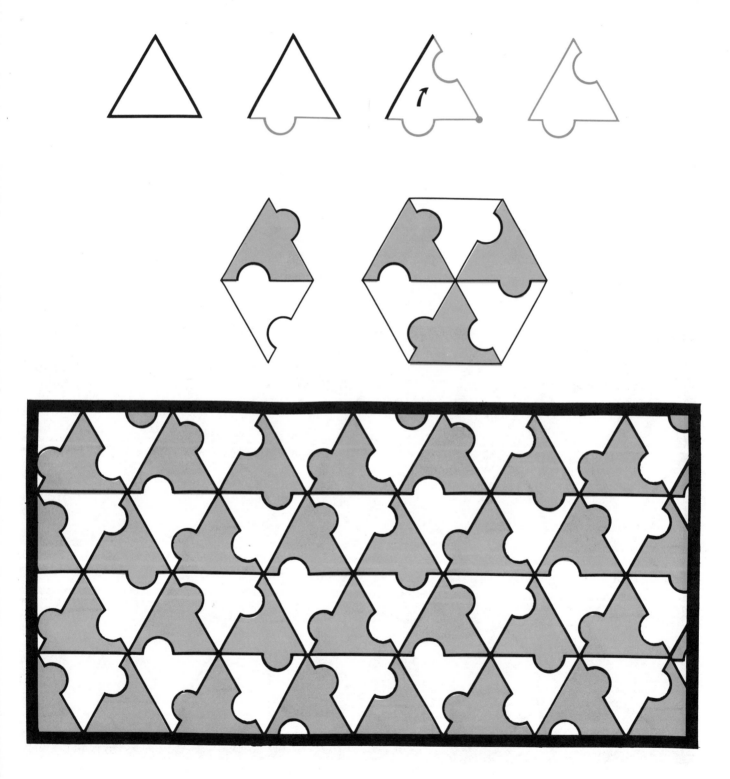

Figure 4-2

The previous two examples of alteration by rotation were illustrated with equilateral triangles. In Figures 4-3 through 4-7, we investigate alterations and rotations with isosceles triangles.

In triangle ABC, $\overline{AB} \cong \overline{AC}$, we first alter $\overline{AC}$, then rotate the alteration to side AB with point A as the center of rotation.

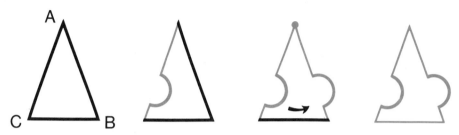

Figure 4-3

We see from the two examples in Figure 4-4 that this shape will not tessellate. In Figure 4-4b, we even tried flipping the shape over.

(a)

(b)

Figure 4-4

65

In Figure 4-5, the alteration of the same basic isosceles triangle is at the midpoint (M) of side AC.

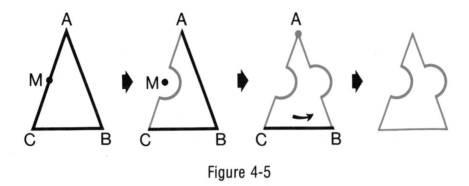

Figure 4-5

In Figure 4-6a, the shape has been rotated 180° but the two shapes do not "fit."
In Figure 4-6b, the shape has been rotated 180°, then reflected. The shapes "fit" together in Figure 4-6c, and form a figure that could be viewed as a parallelogram with a pair of opposite sides altered by a translation.

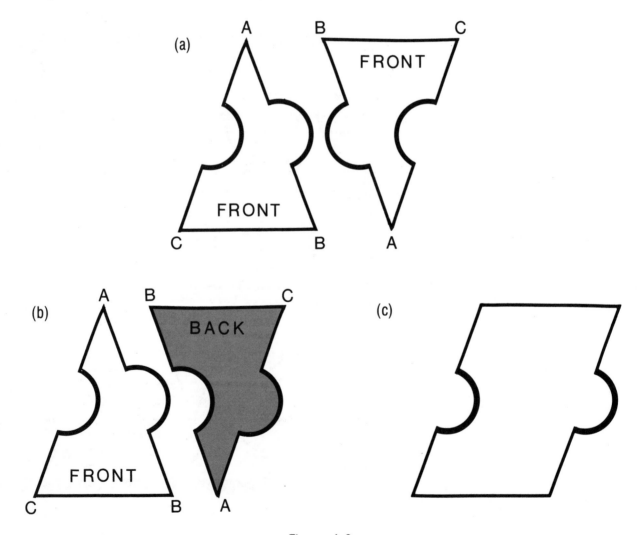

Figure 4-6

When the shape is altered at the midpoint and rotated to a congruent side, it will tessellate, provided alternate shapes are reflected. In Figure 4-7, the shapes that have been flipped are in color.

Figure 4-7

Sometimes a shape and its flipped image are referred to as *right-handed* and *left-handed* shapes. In the previous example, the original shape might be referred to as a *right-handed shape,* and the flipped shape as a *left-handed shape.*

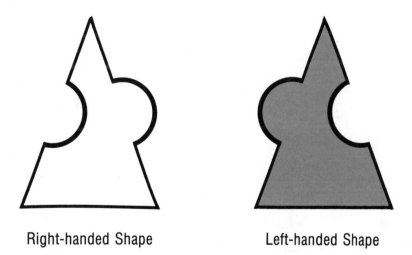

Right-handed Shape          Left-handed Shape

Figure 4-8

# ALTERING TWO OR FOUR SIDES OF A QUADRILATERAL BY ROTATION

Since we are investigating the rotation of an altered side of a polygon to a *congruent* adjacent side, when considering quadrilaterals we need only consider those with congruent adjacent sides. These would include squares, rhombi, and kites.

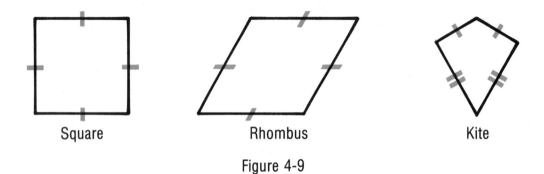

Square          Rhombus          Kite

Figure 4-9

Starting with a square and the alteration of two sides, Figure 4-10 shows that a nonsymmetric alteration creates a tessellation.

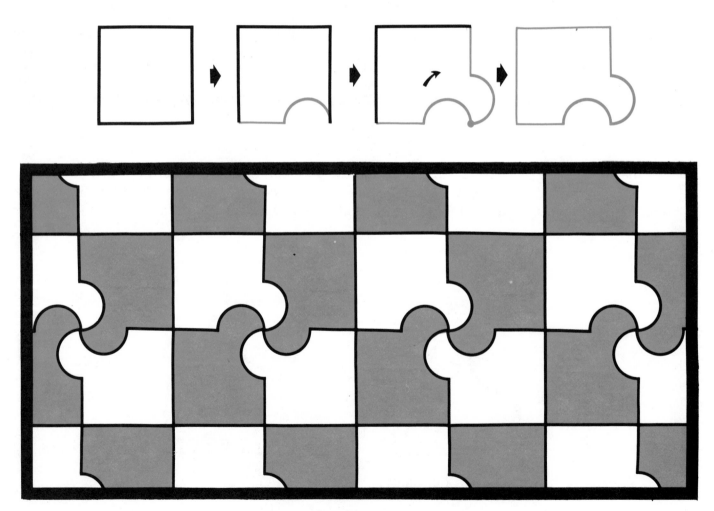

Figure 4-10

The same alteration rotated to the other two sides also tessellates.

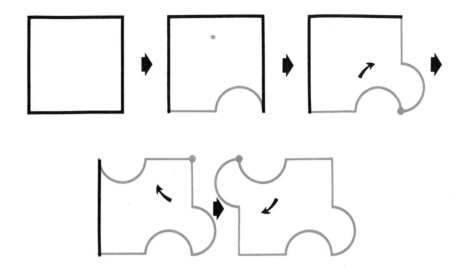

Figure 4-11

A square is a special rhombus. Let's alter two sides of a nonsquare rhombus.

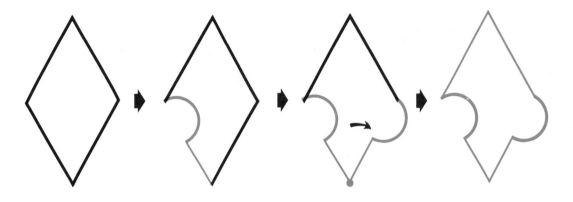

Figure 4-12

Whether the shape is reflected (Figure 4-13a) or not reflected (Figure 4-13b), it does not tessellate.

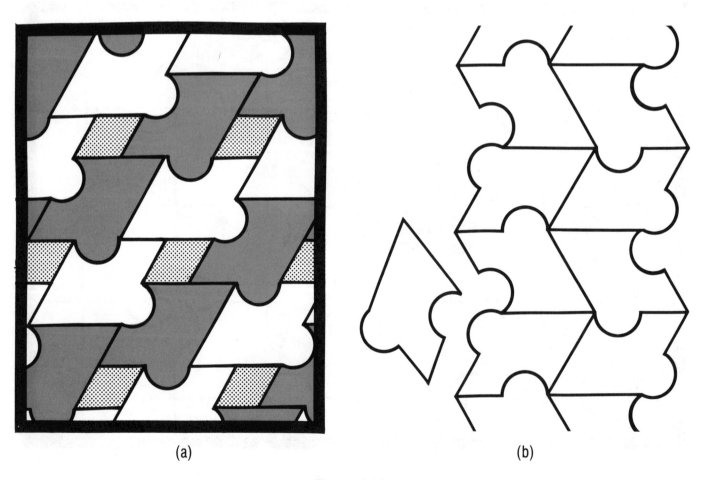

(a)                    (b)

Figure 4-13

If we alter all four sides of the rhombus by rotating the altered side three times, we see that the shape does tessellate (Figure 4-14). The shape has not been flipped.

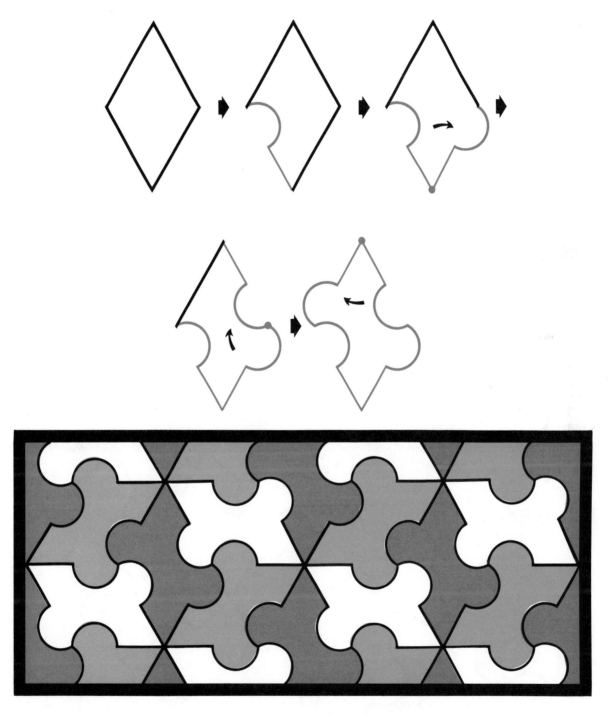

Figure 4-14

Notice that the basic shape creates sixfold symmetry at one point and threefold symmetry at another point.

71

We might conclude from the previous examples of the square and the rhombus that altering four sides of any rhombus by rotation at an endpoint of a side will create a tessellation. The example in Figure 4-15 shows, however, that this *is not* the case. The previous examples were special cases in which angles were 60°, 90°, or 120°.

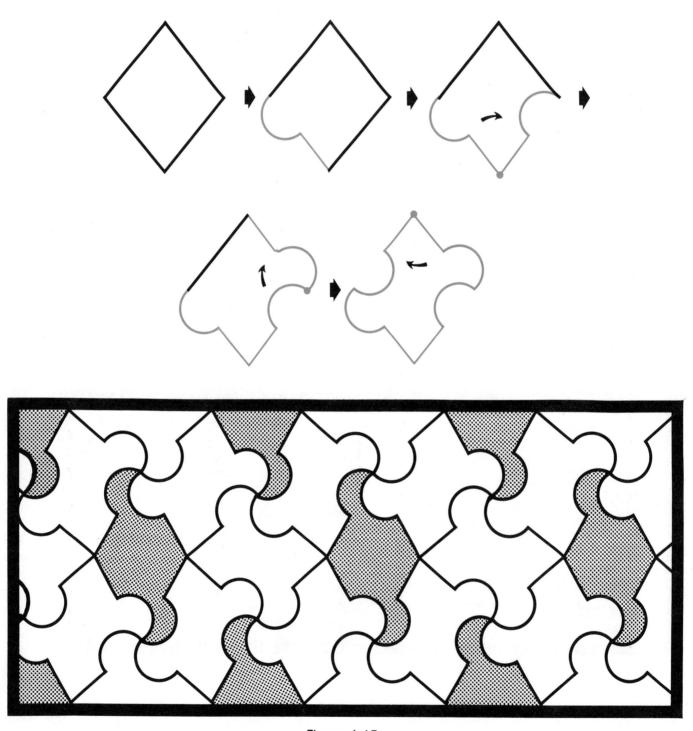

Figure 4-15

An Altered Rhombus That Does Not Tessellate

A rhombus which has had *one* side altered and rotated about an endpoint to an adjacent side will tessellate, provided that: (1) the alteration has point symmetry at the midpoint of the side, or (2) the alteration has line symmetry at the midpoint of the side.

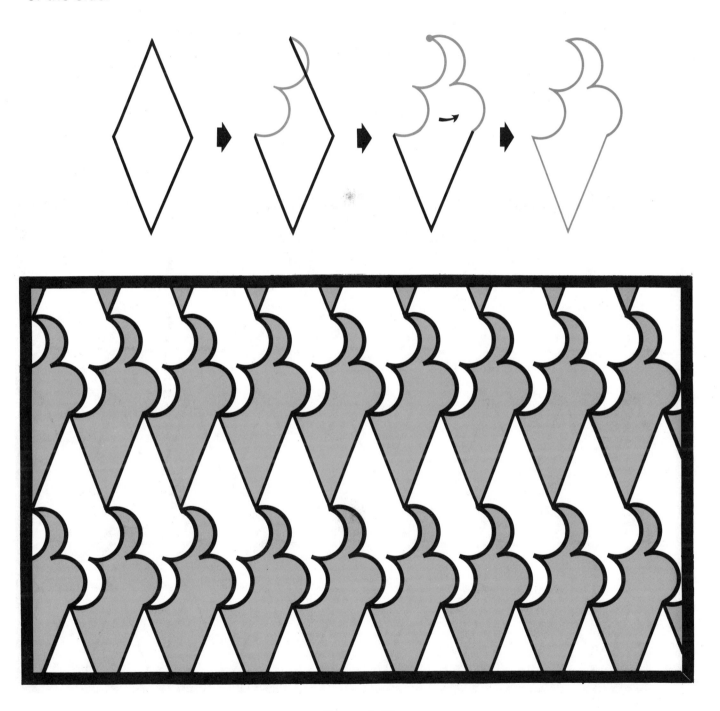

Figure 4-16
Alterations That Are
Line Symmetric
About the Midpoint
(Note left-handed and
right-handed shapes.)

73

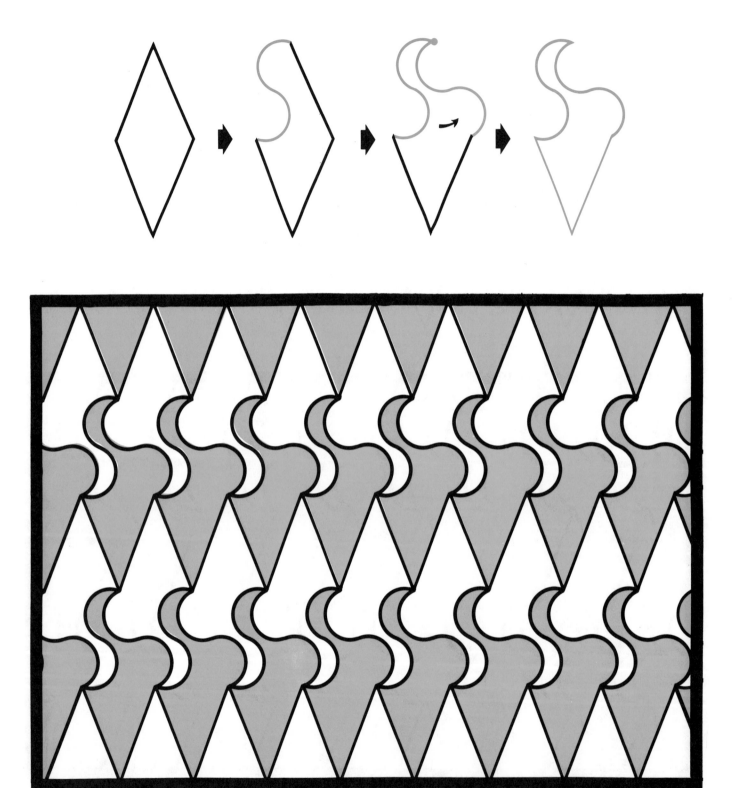

Figure 4-17
Alterations That Are
Point Symmetric
About the Midpoint

If *four* sides of a rhombus are altered by rotation of altered sides at an endpoint, the shape will tessellate, provided that the alterations of the sides have point or line symmetry at the midpoints of the sides.

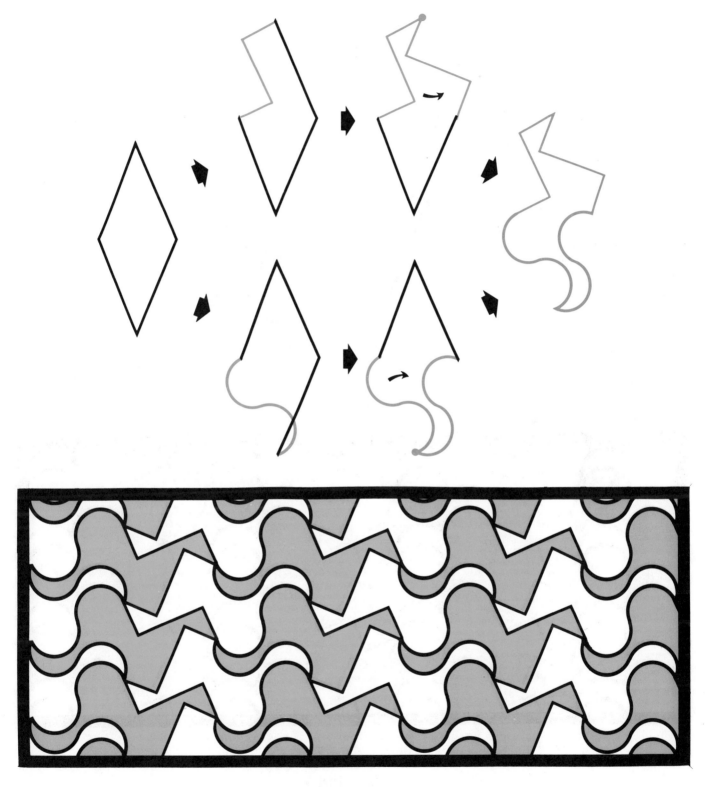

Figure 4-18
Alterations That Are
Point Symmetric
About the Midpoint

Figure 4-19
Alterations That Are
Line Symmetric
About the Midpoint
(Note left-handed
and right-handed shapes)

The example in Figure 4-20 shows an altered shape with two sides having point symmetry at their midpoints and two sides having line symmetry at their midpoints. Right- and left-handed shapes are required.

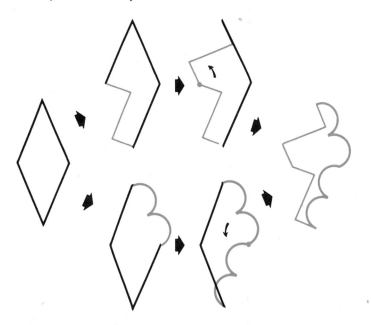

Figure 4-20

You may wish to explore the tessellation possibilities of the kite shape (two pairs of congruent sides) using rotations.

## ALTERING TWO, FOUR, OR SIX SIDES OF A HEXAGON BY ROTATION

Regular hexagons can be altered by rotation of an altered side. Since the sides are all congruent, all alterations could be the same, or two or three different alterations could occur.

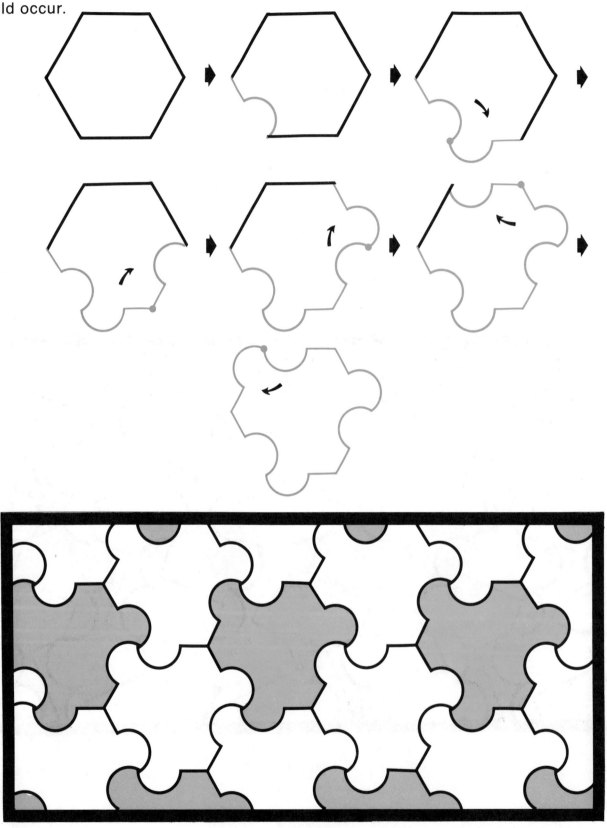

Figure 4-21

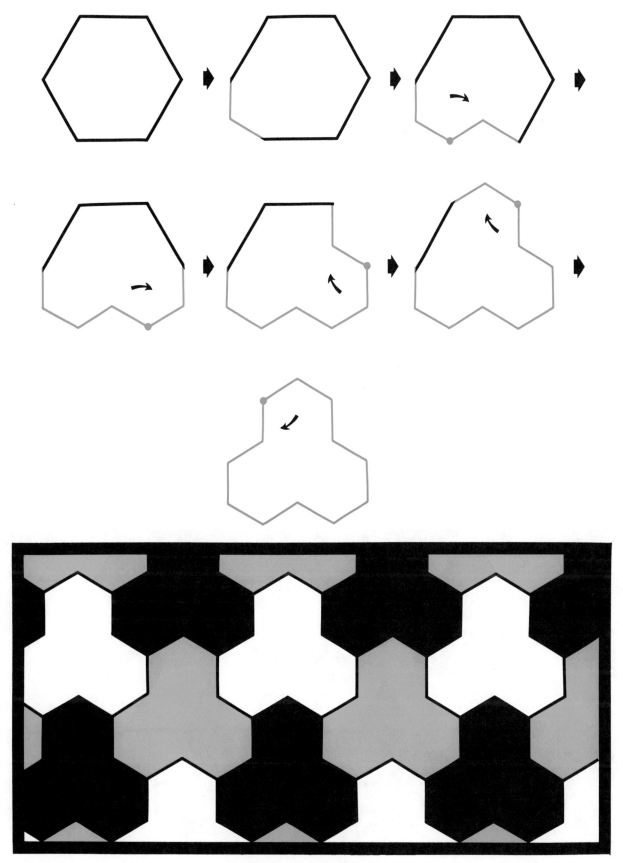

Figure 4-21 (continued)
Examples Showing a
Single Alteration

79

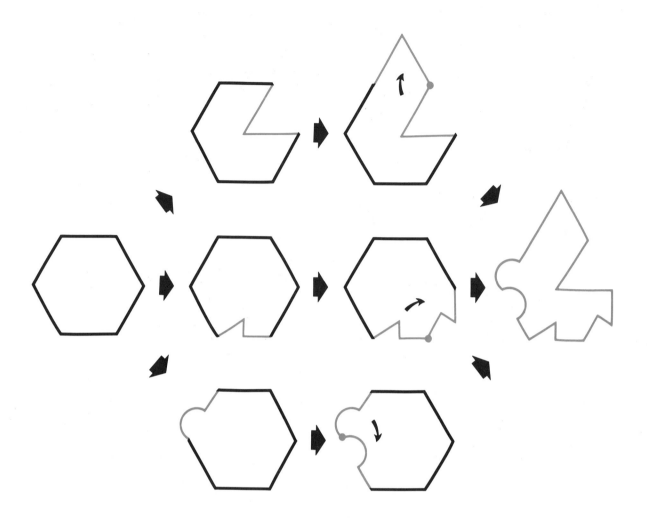

Figure 4-22
Example Showing
Different Alterations

Here is an example of an Escher drawing that was created by altering three sides of a regular hexagon, then rotating the alteration at the endpoint of the side.

M. C. Escher. Study of Regular Division of the Plane with Reptiles. Pen, ink, and watercolor, 1939

Figure 4-23

Figure 4-24 shows the process that Escher may have used to create his drawing of reptiles.

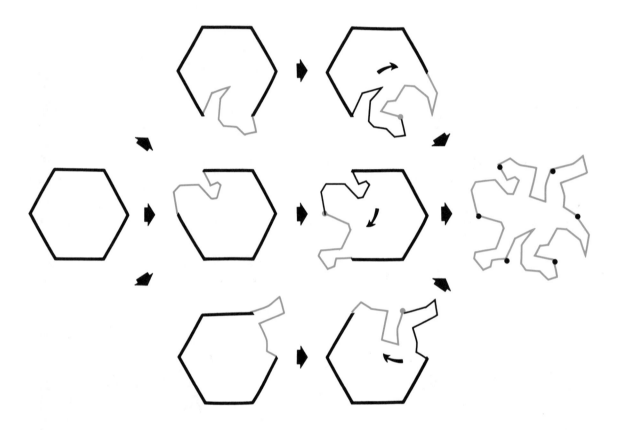

Figure 4-24

As you can see, the technique used in Escher's *Reptiles* was based on a hexagonal tessellation. Sides were altered and rotated about an endpoint.

# ALTERING POLYGONS BY ROTATION OF HALF-SIDES

### ALTERING THE THIRD SIDE OF A TRIANGLE BY ROTATION

We know that if one shape is to completely fill the plane in a tessellation, the areas of each shape in the tessellation must be identical. If we tried to alter each of the three sides of an equilateral triangle by rotation, the new area might not be the same as the original triangle. This is illustrated in Figure 4-25.

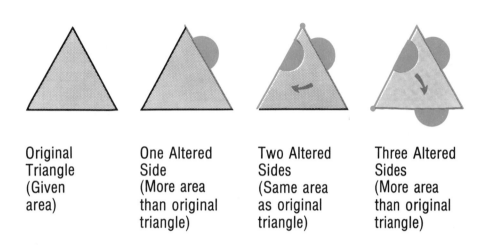

Original
Triangle
(Given
area)

One Altered
Side
(More area
than original
triangle)

Two Altered
Sides
(Same area
as original
triangle)

Three Altered
Sides
(More area
than original
triangle)

Figure 4-25

This shape created by three rotations does not tessellate.

Won't fit

Figure 4-26

When two sides were altered in Figure 4-26, the area added to the triangle by one alteration was subtracted by the second alteration. If the third side of the triangle is to be altered so that the area remains the same, the alteration must subtract as much area from the triangle as it adds. An example of such an alteration is shown in Figure 4-27.

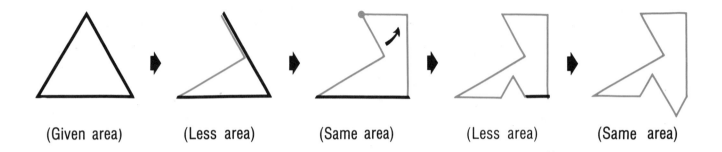

(Given area)     (Less area)     (Same area)     (Less area)     (Same area)

Figure 4-27

It can be seen in Figure 4-28 that this shape will not tessellate by itself, since the sides with the broken straight lines do not coincide.

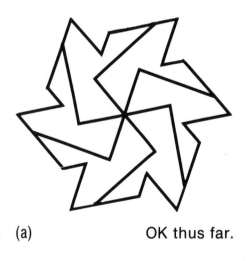

(a)          OK thus far.

(b)          Doesn't tessellate as one shape

Figure 4-28

A special way to create a side that will coincide with itself is to alter one half of the line and then rotate it about its midpoint. This is illustrated in the alteration shown in Figure 4-29. Note that the area of the triangle is not changed by this alteration.

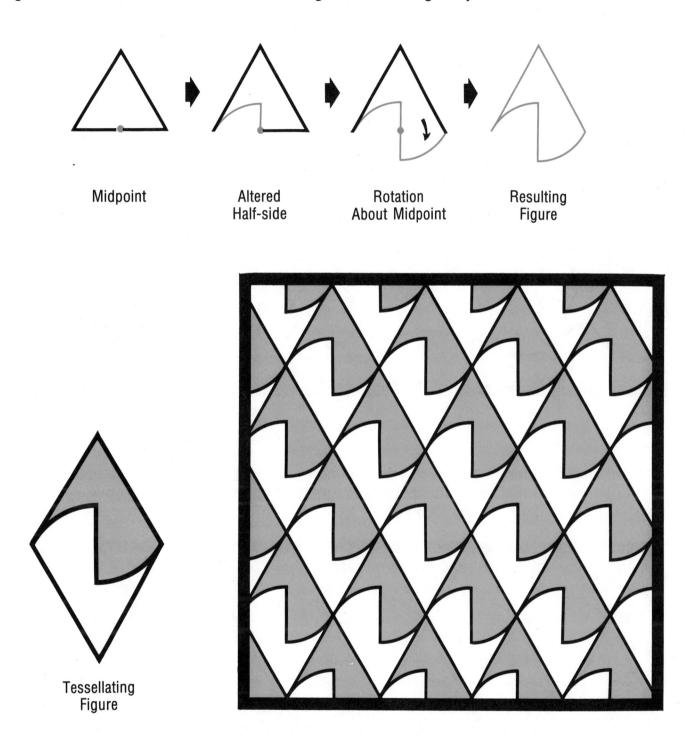

Midpoint  Altered
Half-side  Rotation
About Midpoint  Resulting
Figure

Tessellating
Figure

Figure 4-29

If two sides of a triangle are altered by rotation about an endpoint, and the third side is altered about its midpoint, the altered triangle will tessellate (Figure 4-30).

85

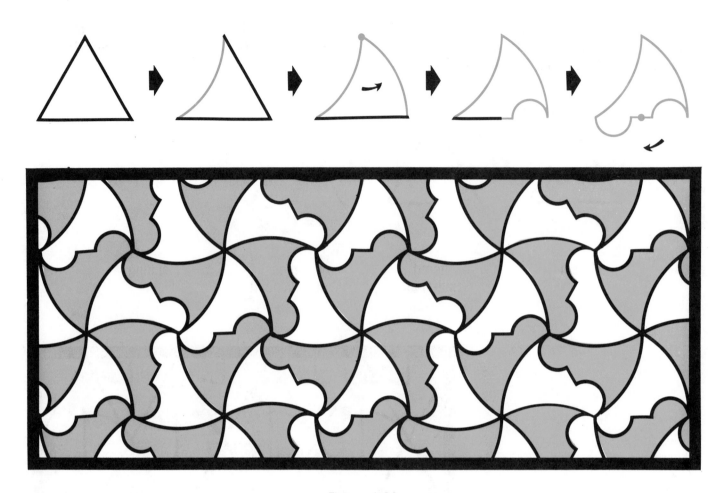

Figure 4-30

If we look at Figure 4-31, which was created by altering one side of a triangle at its midpoint, we see that two figures together form a shape that looks like a parallelogram that has been altered by translation.

Figure 4-31

If we rotate a side of a triangle that has been altered by a rotation about its midpoint, we get a figure that tessellates. It appears to be formed by parallelograms whose opposite sides have been translated.

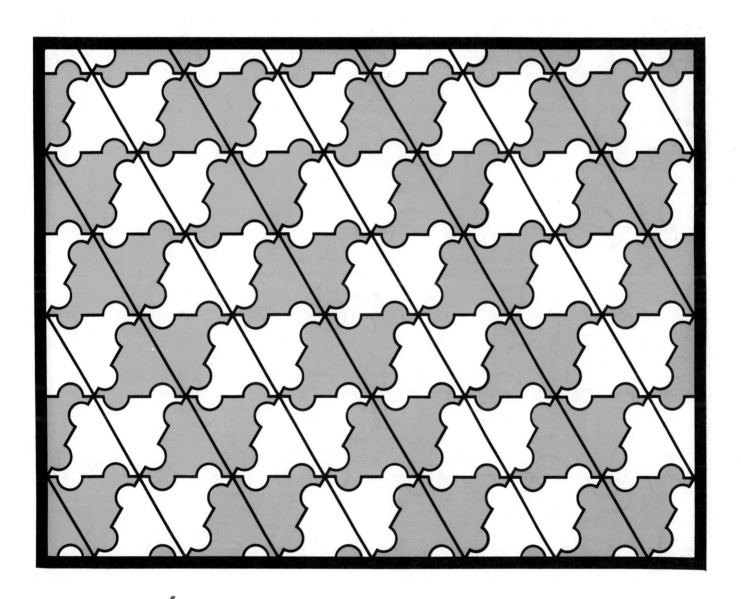

Figure 4-32

Altering all three sides by rotation creates a shape that tessellates. This will only work when the alteration being rotated about the endpoint was created by a rotation about the midpoint of the line. The area of the original triangle remains invariant.

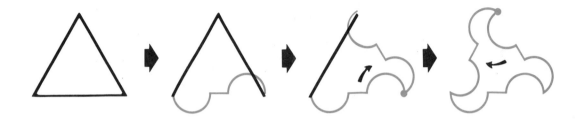

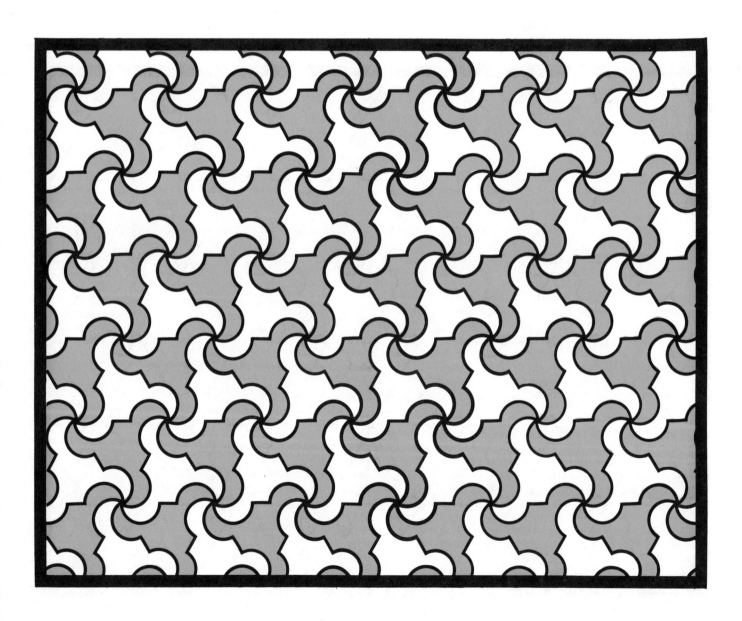

Figure 4-33

The three sides of the triangle need not be altered by the same half-side rotated about the midpoint. The example below shows a figure that tessellates, which was formed by three different half-turn alterations.

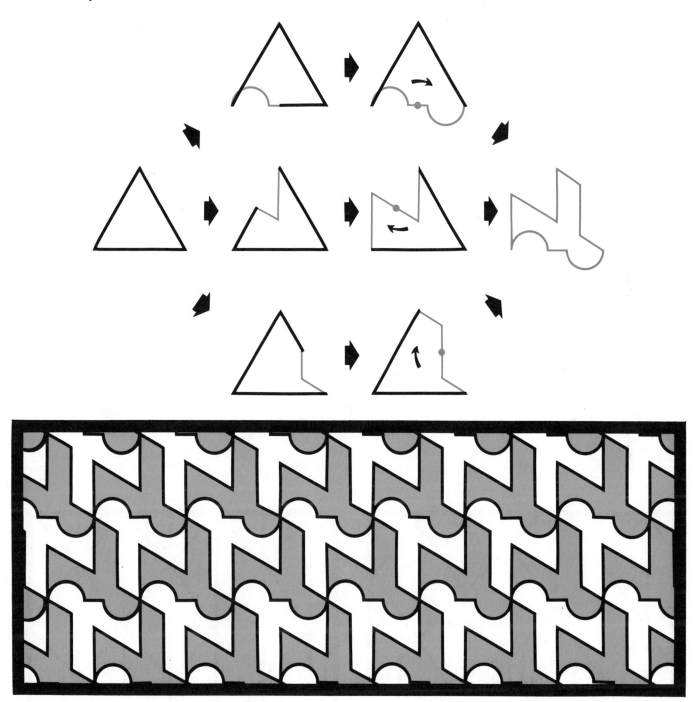

Figure 4-34

When the sides of a tessellating polygon are changed by rotating an alteration about the midpoint of one of its sides, the adjacent or opposite sides need not have the special properties of congruence or parallelism required by translations or rotations about the endpoint of a side.

Thus far we have investigated alterations by rotation about a midpoint of equilateral triangles only. Any triangle will tessellate. Let's see what we get by altering a nonregular, nonisosceles triangle by rotation about the midpoint of its sides.

We recall from Chapter 1 (page 17) that any triangle tessellates in two positions: a kite (by reflection), and a parallelogram (by half-turn). Triangle ABC in Figure 4-35a is shown tessellating in these two positions.

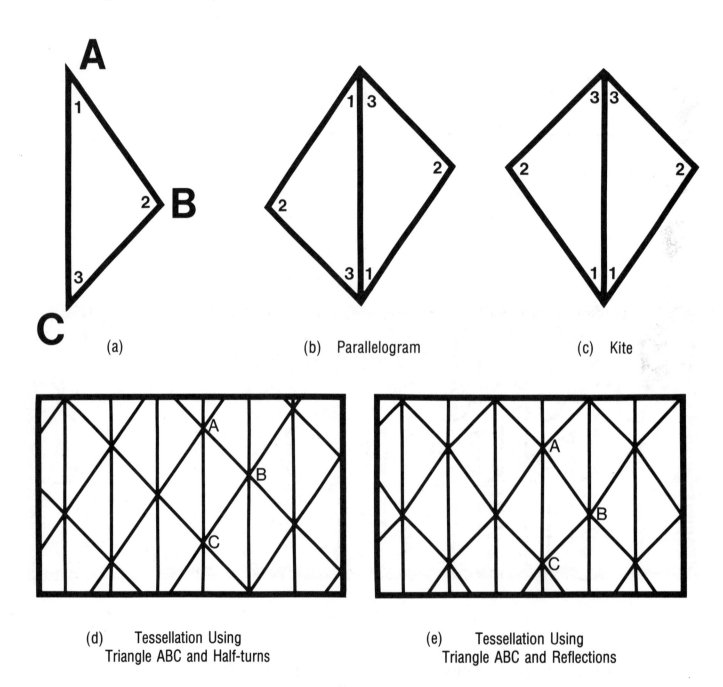

(a)

(b)   Parallelogram

(c)   Kite

(d)   Tessellation Using
Triangle ABC and Half-turns

(e)   Tessellation Using
Triangle ABC and Reflections

Figure 4-35

Altering one half of each of the sides and rotating about the midpoint of each side results in the shape shown in Figure 4-36.

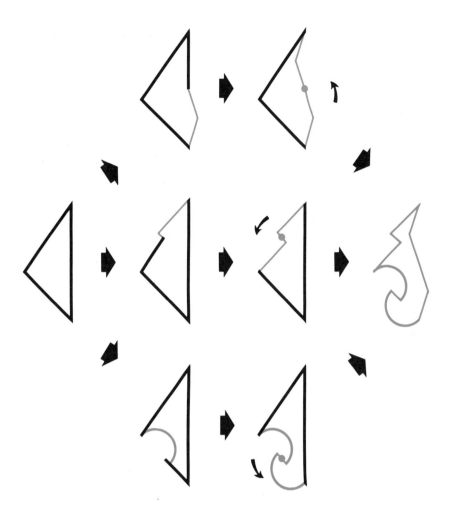

Figure 4-36

Attempting to create a tessellation from the shape reveals that the shape tessellates in the parallelogram configuration (Figure 4-37a) but not in the kite configuration (Figure 4-37b).

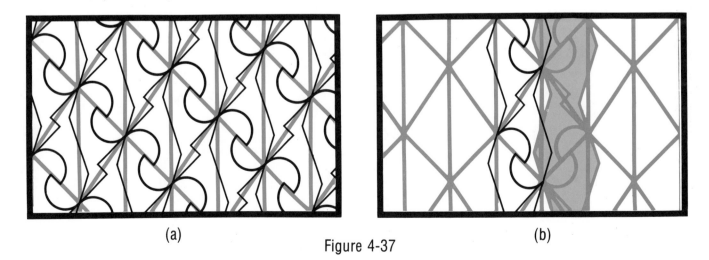

(a)

(b)

Figure 4-37

Note that two of the shapes in the parallelogram base create a combined shape that is equivalent to altering the opposite sides of a parallelogram by translation (Figure 4-38).

Figure 4-38

# ALTERING HALF-SIDES OF QUADRILATERALS BY ROTATION

Here is an example of tessellating quadrilaterals altered by rotation at the midpoint of a side.

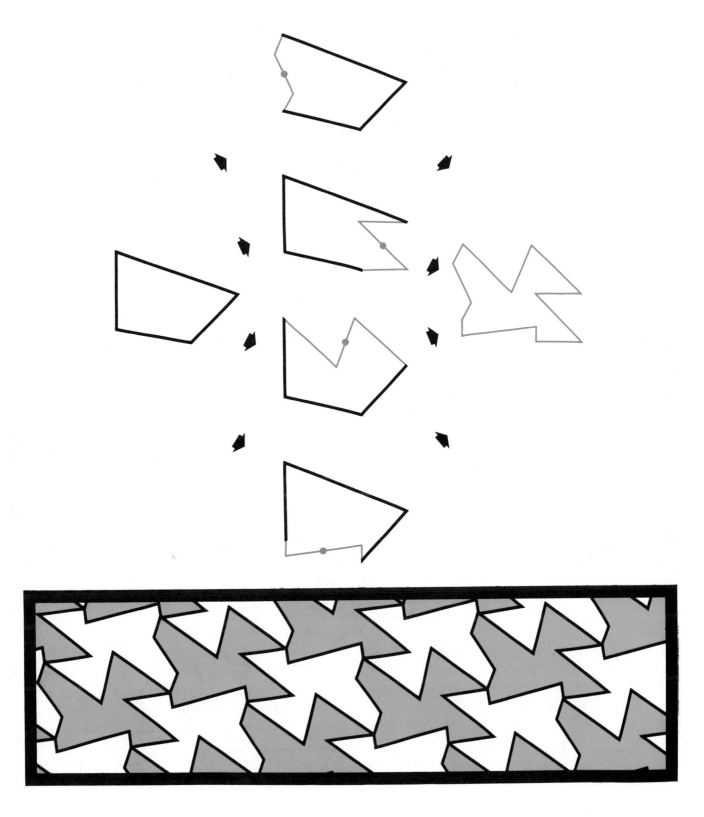

Figure 4-39

## ALTERING HALF-SIDES OF HEXAGONS BY ROTATION
Here is an example of a hexagon whose sides have been altered by rotation at the midpoint.

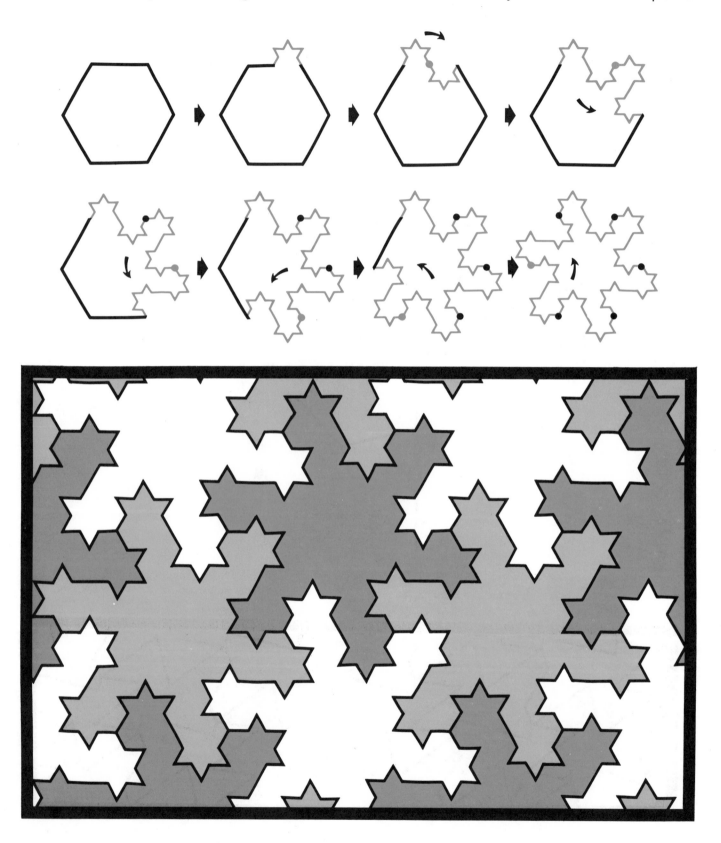

Figure 4-40

# ALTERING POLYGONS BY ROTATIONS OF SIDES AND HALF-SIDES

In the Figure 4-41 drawings, you can see that Escher may have used the technique of altering two sides of an equilateral triangle by rotation from an endpoint and altering the third side by rotation about the midpoint.

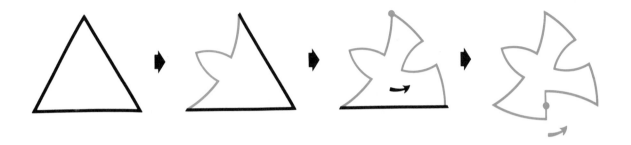

M. C. Escher. Untitled Work

Figure 4-41

Let's try one of our own. Starting by altering one side, we might try something like this.

Figure 4-42

Then let's rotate to an adjacent side.

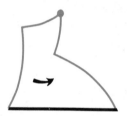

Figure 4-43

Finally, let's change the third straight side by altering one-half the side and rotating about the midpoint.

Figure 4-44

It looks something like a Doberman pinscher, an old-fashioned shoe, or . . .

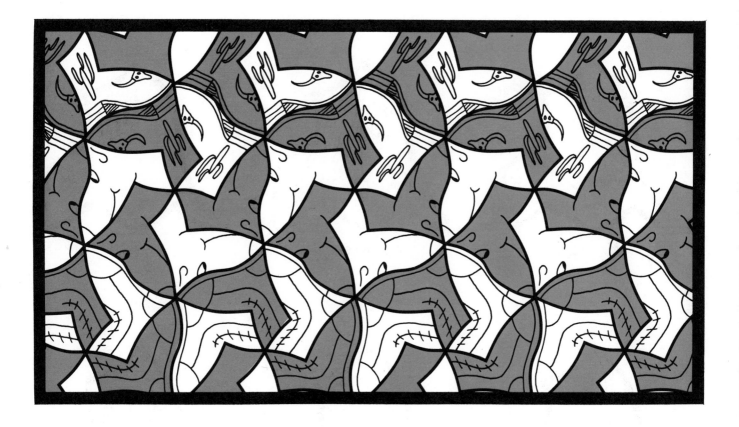

Figure 4-45

Here's another example using the same method of altering an equilateral triangle.

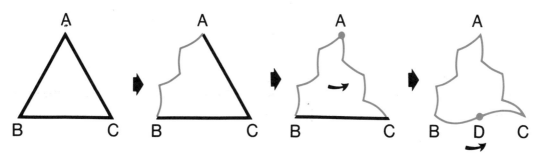

Figure 4-46

Some possible interpretations could be:

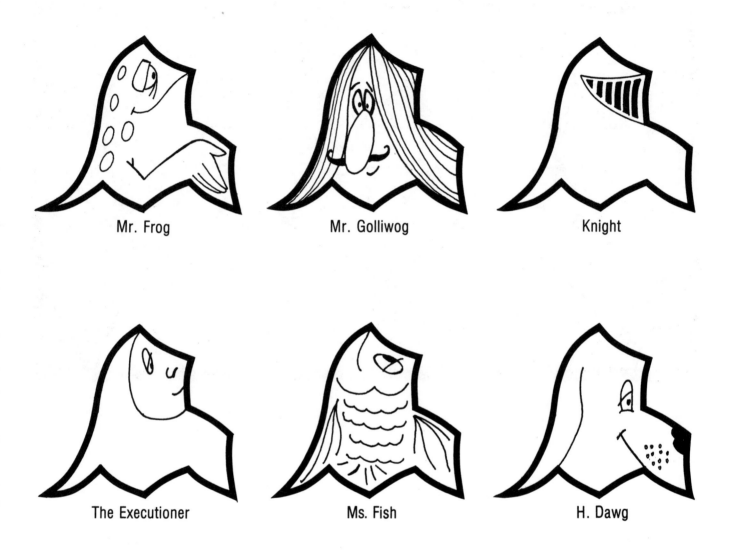

Mr. Frog

Mr. Golliwog

Knight

The Executioner

Ms. Fish

H. Dawg

Figure 4-47

You see that once the mathematics has been applied, the next step depends on your imagination.

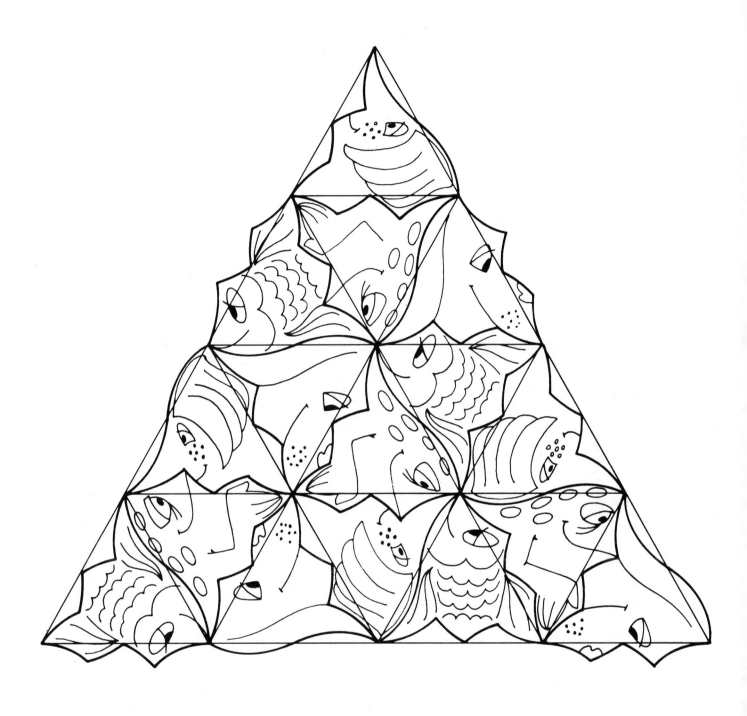

Figure 4-48

If a specific shape is desired in a tessellation of animate figures, possibly one of the three sides of the basic triangle will be altered and not rotated.

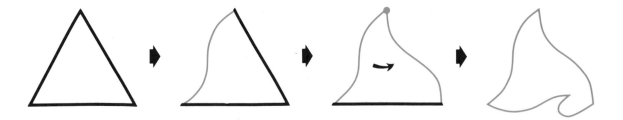

This creates a tessellation of two different shapes.

Figure 4-49

## SUMMARY

In this chapter, we have seen that some tessellating shapes can be created by the rotation of altered sides or half-sides of tessellations.

New tessellating shapes can be created from the regular tessellations by the alteration of a side and the rotation of the altered side about its endpoint to an adjacent side. To create new tessellating shapes from nonregular tessellations, alterations of sides rotated about their endpoints must be point or line symmetric about the midpoint of the side.

Many shapes that tessellate can be changed to new tessellating shapes by alterations that are point symmetric about the midpoints of one or more of their sides.

Some shapes, in order to tessellate by themselves, must be reflected in the plane (flipped over), creating a left- and right-handed shape.

(See worksheets 8-9 through 8-13.)

CHAPTER
FIVE

# ALTERING BY REFLECTION AND ROTATION

## ALTERING TRIANGLES BY REFLECTION

In Chapters 3 and 4, we saw how the sides of tessellating polygons could be altered by translations and rotations to create curved shapes that fill the plane. In this chapter we shall investigate a third transformation, reflection.

Experimenting with an equilateral triangle, we see from the example in Figure 5-1 that if an altered side is reflected about an altitude, a new shape is created and the new area is not the same as the area of the original triangle.

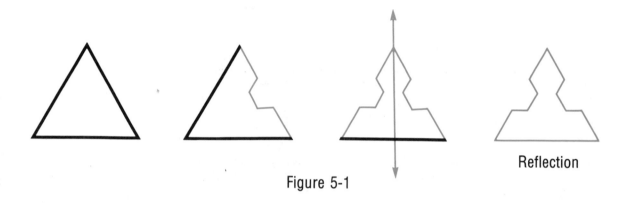

Figure 5-1

Reflection

We can see that the new shape will not tessellate by itself. A second shape is created.

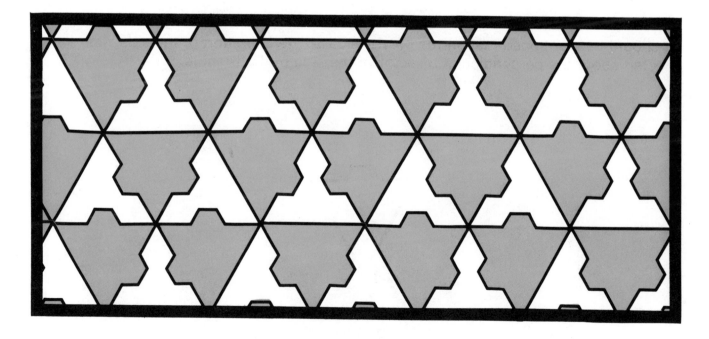

Figure 5-2

105

Reflecting the alteration to the third side of the triangle also creates a two-shape tessellation.

Figure 5-3

It should be mentioned that, in the previous case, the alteration of the side was reflected about the perpendicular bisector of the side of the triangle.

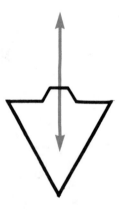

Figure 5-4

In Figure 5-5, the side of an equilateral triangle has been altered. The alteration does not have the special property of being rotated about the midpoint of the line.

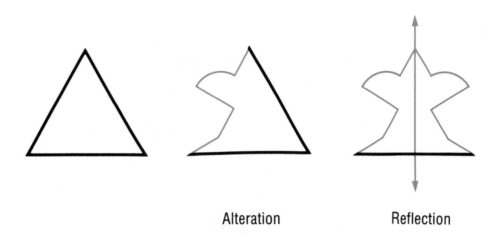

Alteration                    Reflection

Figure 5-5

This shape will not tessellate, even with two shapes.

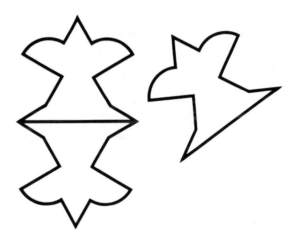

Figure 5-6

## ALTERING TRIANGLES BY REFLECTION AND ROTATION

Experimenting with a shape created by reflecting a random alteration about the altitude will demonstrate the futility of creating a tessellating shape, *even if the entire shape is reflected in the plane.*

In Figure 5-6, we could not get the curves of the shapes to "fit with each other." This is not the case, however, if the altered curve is reflected, *then rotated* 180 degrees about the midpoint of the line.

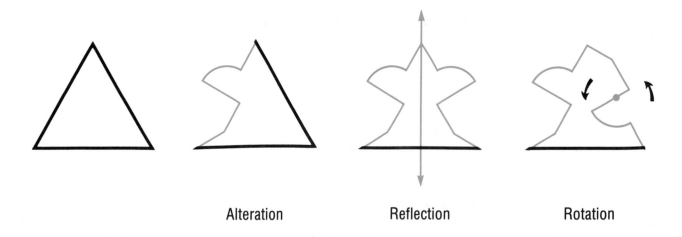

| Alteration | Reflection | Rotation |

Figure 5-7

We can see in Figure 5-8 that translating and rotating the new shape will not create a "fit" with itself.

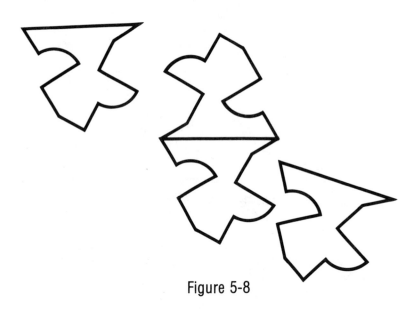

Figure 5-8

*However,* if we reflect the shape (flip it over), it will fit.

Figure 5-9

It will tessellate the plane by itself.

Figure 5-10

Trace the outline of a shaded shape in Figure 5-10. Move the traced outline to coincide with another shaded shape. Try making the shape coincide with an unshaded shape. Flip your traced outline over and try fitting it to the unshaded shape. Try fitting it to the shaded shape.

Another simple example of a shape created by a *reflection and rotation* is shown in Figure 5-11.

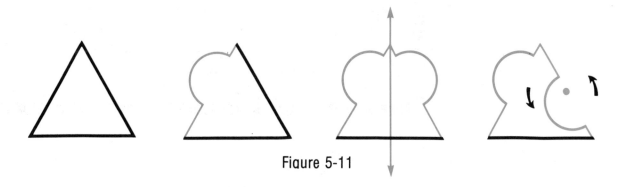

Figure 5-11

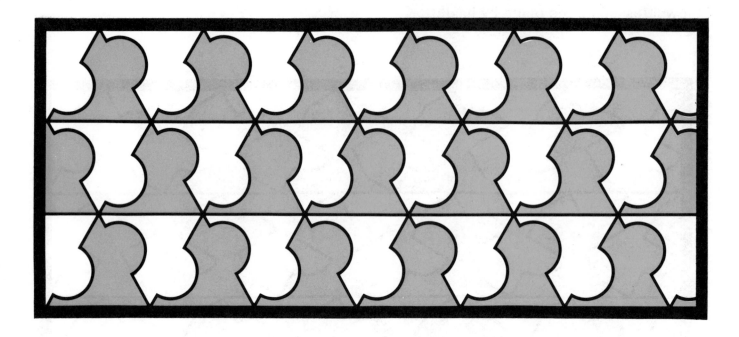

Figure 5-11 (continued)

If the shape in Figure 5-11 could not be reflected, it would tessellate as shown in Figure 5-12. Two new shapes would appear in the uncovered areas, a triangle and a hexagon.

Figure 5-12

The third side of a triangle can be altered as shown in Figure 5-13. Curve AB is reflected, becoming curve CB. Curve CB is rotated 180 degrees about the midpoint of the side. One-half the third side is altered (curve AM). Then curve AM is reflected at the midpoint. Finally, the reflection of curve AM is rotated 180 degrees on the half-side.

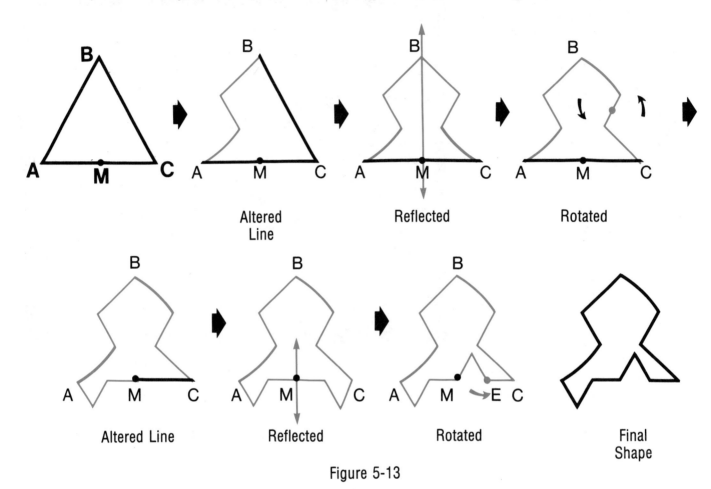

Figure 5-13

We can see in Figures 5-14 and 5-15 that the shape tessellates if it is reflected in the plane.

Figure 5-14

111

The shaded shapes have been reflected in the plane to create the tessellation.

Figure 5-15

Notice that the underlying basis for the tessellation has shifted so that not all of the triangle sides coincide.

Figure 5-16

These birds were created by the technique explained above.

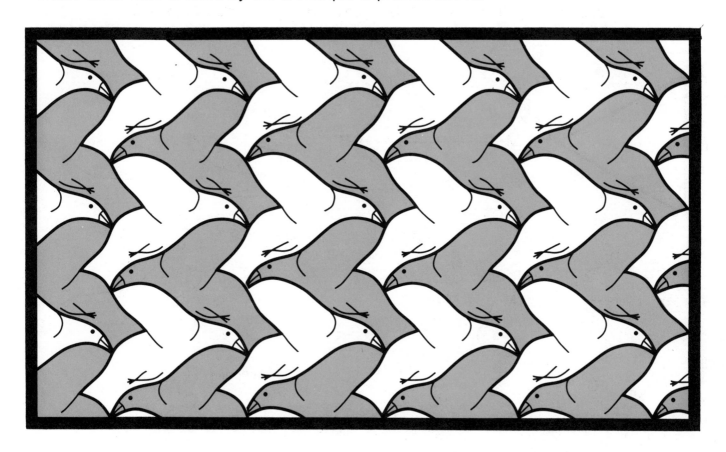

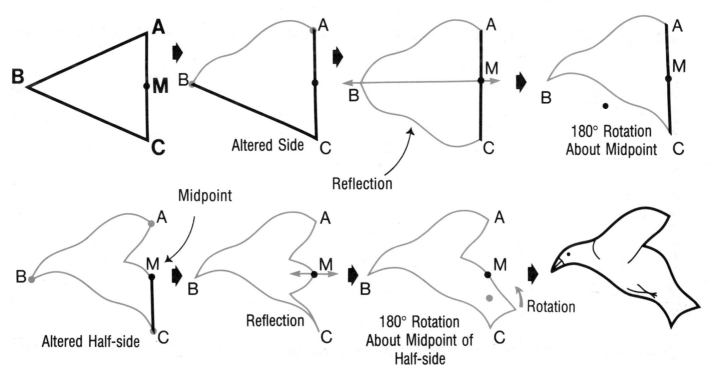

Figure 5-17

Figure 5-18 shows another example of the same technique. $\overline{AB}$ is altered, and altered $\overline{AB}$ is reflected about $\overline{BM}$ to $\overline{BC}$ (Figure 5-18b). The reflection at $\overline{BC}$ is then rotated about the midpoint of $\overline{BC}$ (Figure 5-18c). $\overline{AM}$ is altered, and altered $\overline{AM}$ is reflected about point M (Figure 5-18d). The reflection at $\overline{MC}$ is then rotated about the midpoint of $\overline{MC}$ (Figure 5-18e).

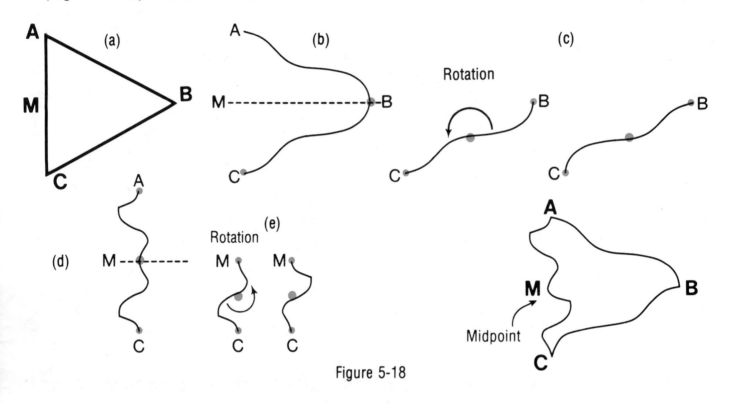

Figure 5-18

This shape produces the Saint Bernard tessellation shown in Figure 5-19.

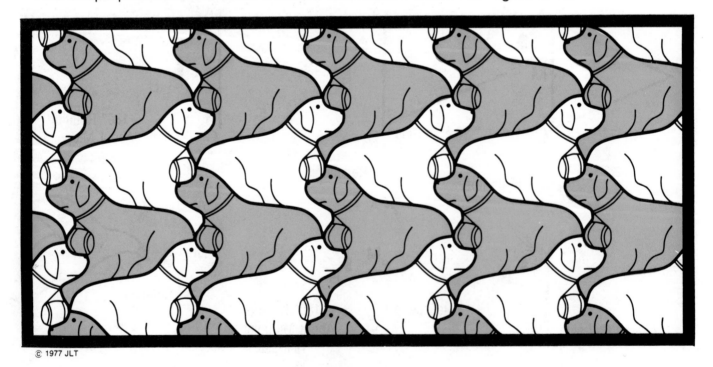

© 1977 JLT

Figure 5-19

# ALTERING RHOMBI BY REFLECTION AND ROTATION

A quick test of the reflection-rotation technique on a rhombus verifies that it creates a tessellation.

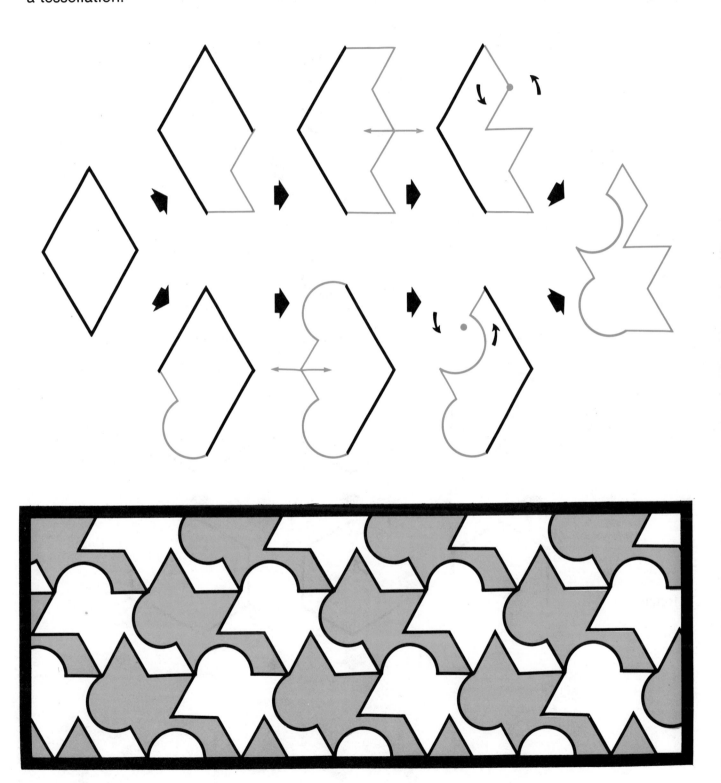

Figure 5-20

# ALTERING HEXAGONS BY REFLECTION AND ROTATION

The hexagonal shape shown in Figure 5-21 has been created by reflecting alterations to an adjacent side, then rotating the reflection about the midpoint of the side. The area of the hexagon remains invariant. However, as can be seen in Figure 5-22, the newly created shape does not tessellate even if the shape is reflected in the plane.

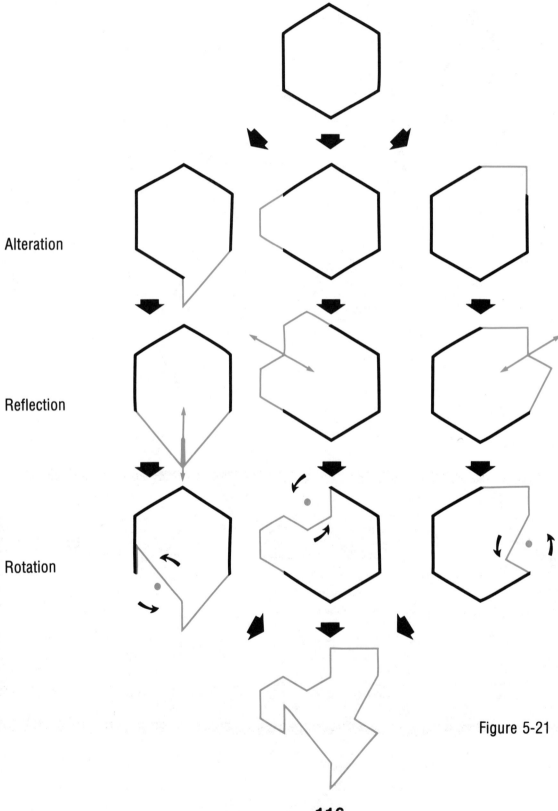

Alteration

Reflection

Rotation

Figure 5-21

116

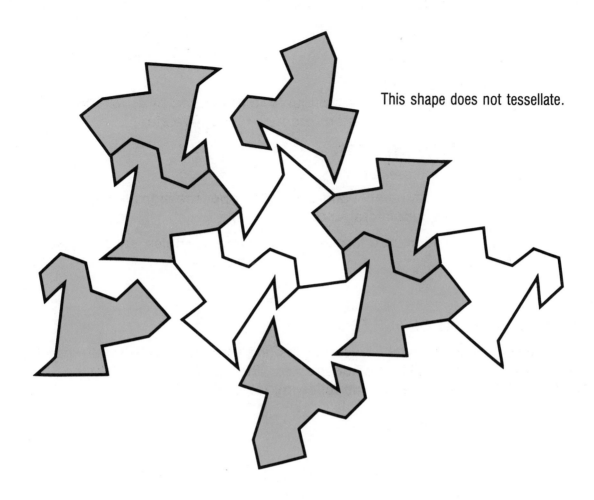

This shape does not tessellate.

Figure 5-22

## SUMMARY

In this chapter we have seen that, in certain polygons, reflecting an altered side to an adjacent, congruent side and then rotating that reflection about the midpoint of the side creates a shape that tessellates. This is true of isosceles and equilateral triangles, kites, and rhombi. It is necessary to reflect the new shape if it is to tessellate by itself.

Furthermore, if an additional side is altered (in the method described above) in such a way as to have point symmetry about its midpoint, that shape will tessellate.

(See worksheets 8-14 through 8-17.)

# SUMMARY OF CHAPTERS ONE THROUGH FIVE

## POLYGONS THAT TESSELLATE
1. Every triangle tessellates
   - as part of a parallelogram configuration (produced by a half-turn).
   - as part of a kite configuration (produced by a reflection).
2. Every quadrilateral tessellates.
3. Some pentagons tessellate.
4. Every hexagon with parallel and congruent opposite sides tessellates (produced by a quadrilateral and a half-turn).

The regular tessellations are formed by equilateral triangles, squares, and regular hexagons.

## TRANSFORMATIONS OF ALTERED SIDES

By altering sides of tessellating polygons and transforming the altered sides, new tessellating shapes can be constructed. The transformations that we considered are summarized in the following table.

## SUMMARY OF TRANSFORMATIONS
## THAT RESULT IN NEW TESSELLATIONS WHEN APPLIED TO TESSELLATING POLYGONS

| TRANSFORMATION / POLYGON | 1 TRANSLATION of an Altered Side to the Parallel, Congruent Opposite Side | 2 ROTATION of an Altered Side at Its Endpoint to a Congruent, Adjacent Side | 3 ROTATION of an Altered Half-side 180° About Its Endpoint (Midpoint of the Side) | 4 REFLECTION of an Altered Side Rotated 180° About the Midpoint of the Reflected Side | 5 REFLECTION of an Altered Half-side Rotated 180° About the Midpoint of the (Adjacent) Half-side |
|---|---|---|---|---|---|
| **TRIANGLES** | | | | | |
| • Scalene Triangle | No | No | Yes | No | Yes† |
| • Isosceles Triangle | No | Yes*†† | Yes | Yes | Yes† |
| • Equilateral Triangle | No | Yes†† | Yes†† | Yes†† | Yes† |
| **QUADRILATERALS** | | | | | |
| • Any Quadrilateral | No | No | Yes | No | No |
| • Kite | No | No | Yes | Yes | No |
| • Parallelogram | Yes | No | Yes | No | Yes† |
| • Rhombus | Yes | Yes* | Yes | Yes | Yes† |
| • Square | Yes | Yes | Yes | Yes | Yes† |
| **HEXAGONS** | | | | | |
| • Hexagon With Congruent and Parallel Opposite Sides | Yes | No | Yes | No | No |
| • Regular Hexagon | Yes | Yes | Yes | No | No |

*If the alteration is point symmetric or line symmetric about the midpoint of the side
†One side only
††Two sides only
Note: Some combinations of the five methods described above will result in tessellations.

CHAPTER SIX

# ANALYZING ESCHER'S TESSELLATIONS

In Chapters 3, 4, and 5, we learned how tessellating triangles, parallelograms, and hexagons can be altered to create animate figures that tessellate the plane. These shapes were created by altering one or more sides of the polygon and then applying transformations or combinations of the transformations—translations, rotations, and reflections—to the altered side.

In this chapter we shall analyze four of Escher's drawings. Although we have no way of knowing specifically what process Escher used to create these drawings, it is fun to speculate about some techniques that he might have used.

M. C. Escher. *Day and Night.* Woodcut, 1938

Figure 6-1

First, let's look at the duck pattern that is the basis for Escher's famous *Day and Night* woodcut.

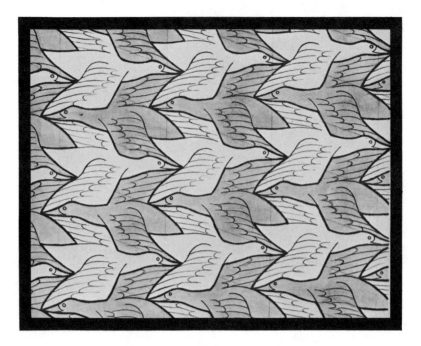

M. C. Escher. Study of Regular Division of the Plane with Birds.
India ink, pencil, and watercolor, 1938

Figure 6-2

The basis for this drawing was apparently a parallelogram. We could select a number of key points to represent the vertices of the parallelogram as we begin to analyze the drawing. In fact, you see in Figure 6-3 three possible choices for a basic tessellating shape.

(a)                    (b)                    (c)

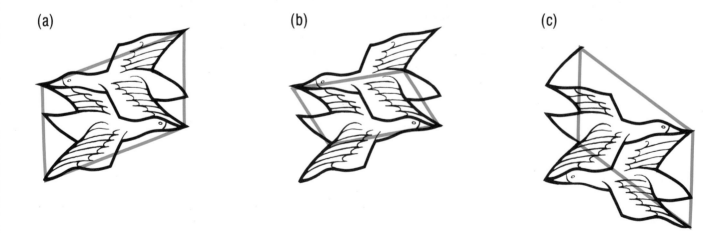

Figure 6-3

In Figure 6-4, curve AB translates to curve DC. However, curves BC and AD can not be made to coincide through translation, rotation, reflection, or any combination of those transformations. It is also obvious that the area of the parallelogram is greater than the area of the two birds combined. Therefore, parallelogram ABCD is not the polygonal tessellation basis for the drawing.

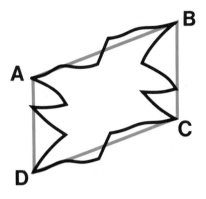

Figure 6-4

Figure 6-5 contains a transformation of curve EH to curve FG. Alterations of sides EF and GH both add area to parallelogram EFGH; hence, the area of the two birds combined is greater than the area of the parallelogram. Therefore, parallelogram EFGH is not the polygonal tessellation basis for the drawing.

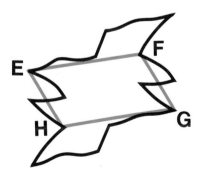

Figure 6-5

Figure 6-6 was discovered when we looked for lines that translate. Curve IJ translates to curve LK while curve IL translates to curve JK; hence, the area of the parallelogram remains invariant. Therefore, parallelogram IJKL is the basis for the design. Notice that the alterations of sides IJ and IL coincide at MI. Escher used this technique in a number of drawings.

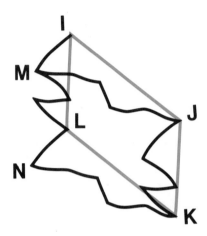

Figure 6-6

Notice that the ducks were made nearly identical by the reflection and rotation of curve MJ to create curve JN. Although curve NK is the translation of MJ, it is also very close to being its own line in reflection. Test this with tracing paper.

If you have some doubts about your artistic talents, it may be comforting to you to know that the drawing below was one of Escher's first attempts at tessellating the plane with animate figures.

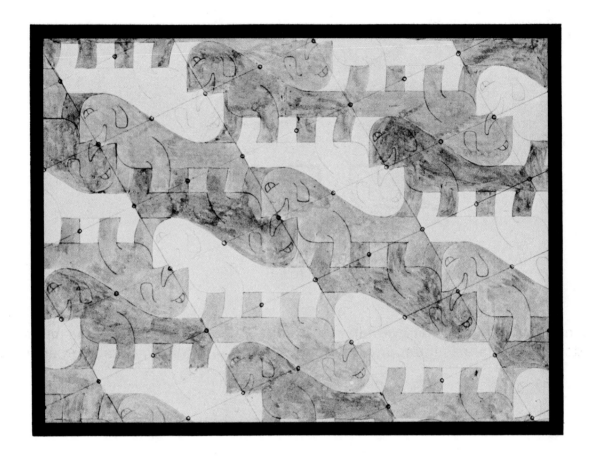

M. C. Escher. Study of Regular Division of the Plane with Imaginary Animals.
Pencil and watercolor, 1926 or 1927

Figure 6-7

Each animal in Figure 6-7 can be thought of as a quadrilateral ABCD (Figure 6-8) whose sides have been altered by rotation around the midpoint of the side (Figure 6-9). Notice that $\overline{BC}$ and $\overline{CD}$ overlap near C.

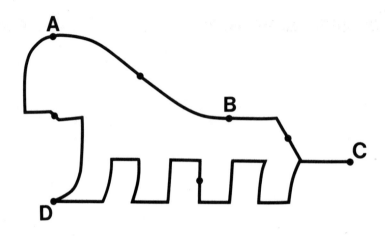

Figure 6-8

It is interesting to note that by rotating the entire figure around each of the midpoints of the sides, one generates the four neighboring figures. Try this with tracing paper.

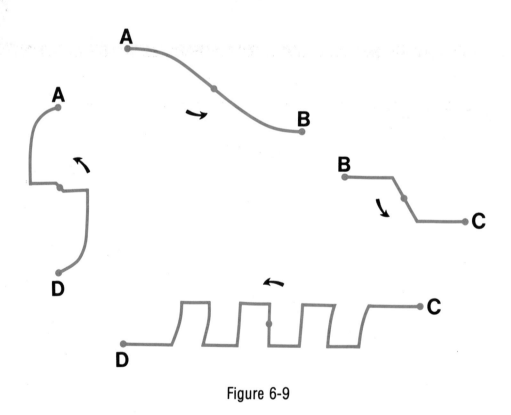

Figure 6-9

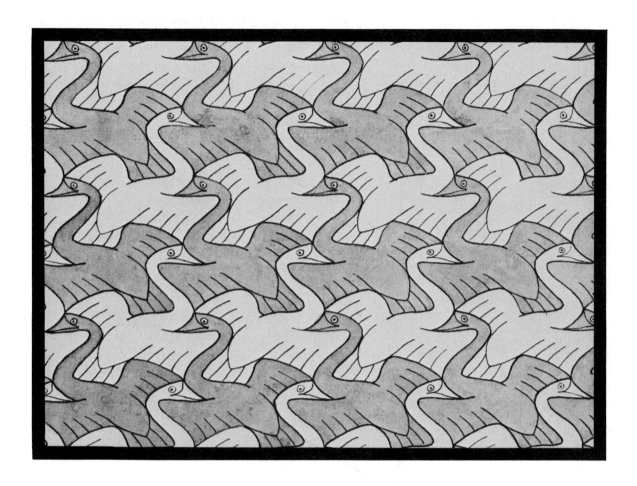

M. C. Escher. Study of Regular Division of the Plane with Birds.
India ink and watercolor, 1955

Figure 6-10

The tessellating geese pictured in Figure 6-10 were formed by the same reflection and rotation process that was used to create the St. Bernard tessellation in Chapter 5 (Figure 5-19).

Starting with quadrilateral ABCD (Figure 6-11), $\overline{AB}$ was altered, then reflected and rotated to form $\overline{BC}$. $\overline{AD}$ was altered, then reflected and rotated to form $\overline{DC}$.

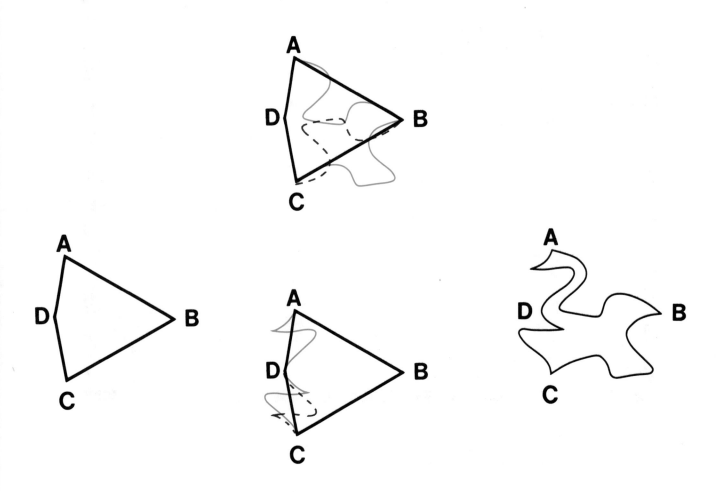

Figure 6-11

Escher gave some insights into the development of the three-dimensional character in Figure 6-12 with his two-dimensional drawing of the same character in Figure 6-13.

Figure 6-12

M. C. Escher. *Cycle.* Lithograph, 1938

Figure 6-13

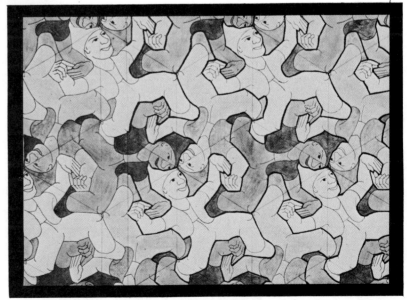

M. C. Escher. Study of Regular Division of the Plane with Human Figures. India ink, pencil, and watercolor, 1938

**131**

The basic cells for the drawing are distorted hexagons (Figure 6-14).

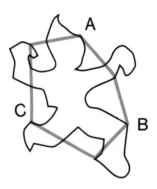

Figure 6-14

The edges were altered in pairs by rotation around three of the vertices as shown in Figure 6-15.

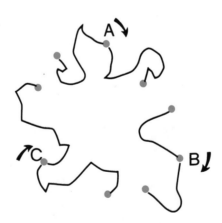

Figure 6-15

These three points, on the forehead, the knee, and the ankle, appear in the tessellation as centers of threefold rotational symmetry (Figure 6-16).

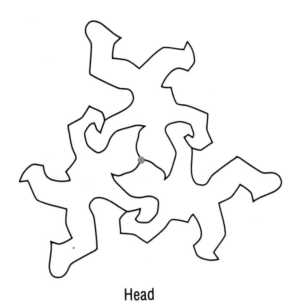

Head

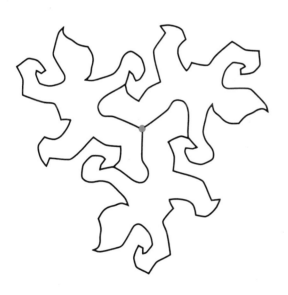

Knee

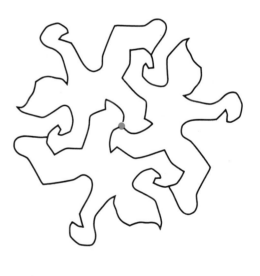

Ankle

Figure 6-16

One can discover more about Escher's drawings by analyzing them with tracing paper. In this book our exploration of his work is obviously limited. The bibliography on page 189 lists a number of books that contain prints of Escher drawings, which provide interesting opportunities to analyze and discover additional Escher techniques.

CHAPTER
SEVEN

In the previous chapters we have explained the mathematics in creating simple two-dimensional animated shapes that tessellate. Understanding the mathematics is the first requirement; the use of your imagination is the second requirement. Finally, a third factor that is not absolutely necessary but that helps somewhat is artistic ability. Many of us need to rely mainly on the mathematics and imagination since our artistic training and experience is limited.

Escher, of course, was a draftsman and artist by trade. However, as we see in one of his first tessellating drawings on page 127, his beginning drawings were not great works of art.

## USING IMAGINATION

In order to create animated figures that are recognizable, you first experiment with the alteration of a triangle, parallelogram, or hexagon. Looking at the new figure, you try to visualize boundaries of familiar objects. Once you have an idea as to what the shape might represent, the next step is to begin modifying the shape to look more like what you imagine it to be.

An example of this process is illustrated in the following figures. A tessellating hexagon has been modified by translating some simple alterations of opposite sides.

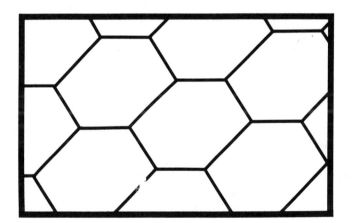 

Figure 7-1

Now, the imagination is required. What does the outline remind you of?

Figure 7-2

Nothing? Try again. Turn it in several directions. Ask a friend for suggestions.

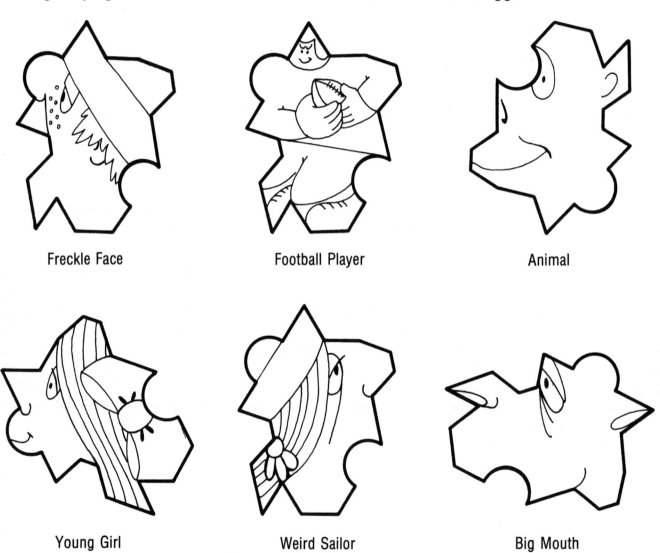

Freckle Face          Football Player          Animal

Young Girl          Weird Sailor          Big Mouth

Figure 7-3

Once you have a general idea, the next step is to modify the alterations to look a bit more like what you want the shape to look like. Let's illustrate what we mean by working with the football player idea.

The player is running. The triangular hat needs to be changed to a helmet. The legs need to look more like legs. The arm on the left needs to be more like the one on the right . . . and so on.

Figure 7-4

We carve away a bit and, presto, we see a backfield that any pro team would like to have.

Figure 7-5

## USING SPECIAL TECHNIQUES

The previous example demonstrated the technique of creating a tessellating shape by visualizing an animated object from the shape and finally modifying it to create a desired result. A completely different approach is to start with a design in mind and to use your knowledge of the mathematics of tessellation to create a figure that tessellates.

Let's consider the football player again. You may have seen a photograph or an artist's sketch that could be a beginning. The general outline of what you have in mind might be in a more triangular shape like the one in Figure 7-6.

Figure 7-6

The shape is more like an isosceles right triangle than an equilateral triangle. The football player in Figure 7-7 resulted from drawing curve AM and rotating and reflecting it to curve CM, then drawing curve AB and rotating and reflecting it to curve BC. Note that the overlapping of curves AM and AB resulted in the rounded shape of the helmet.

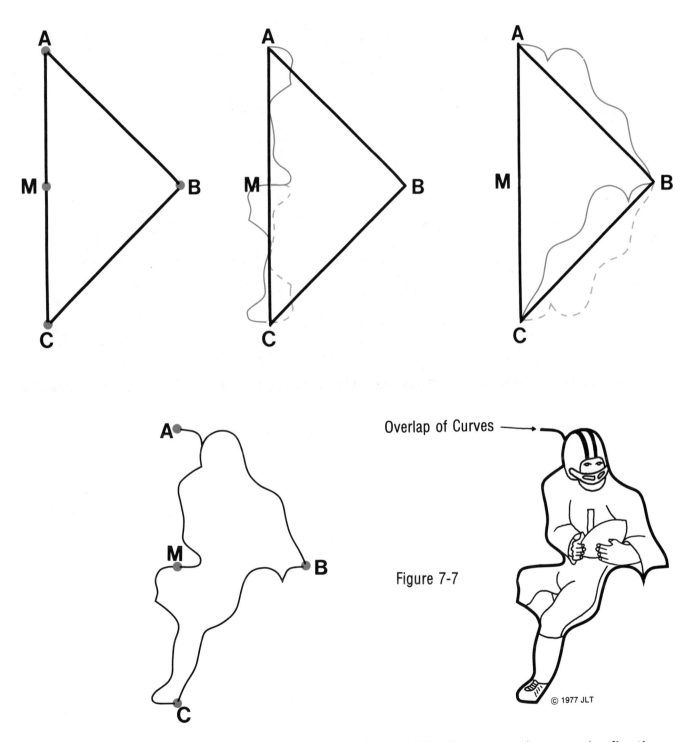

Overlap of Curves

Figure 7-7

© 1977 JLT

This creation was the result of a number of trials, modifications, rotations, and reflections.

The tessellating players are shown in Figure 7-8.

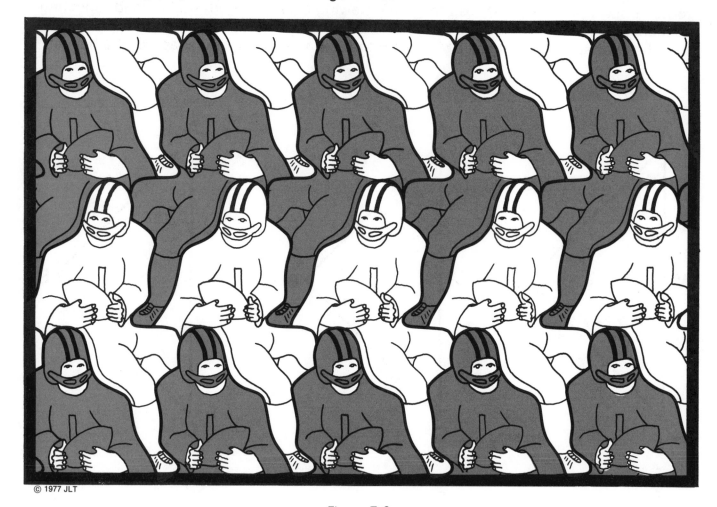

Figure 7-8

The overlapping of lines is a good technique to help you achieve shapes that you want. When drawing two curves, say one from point A to point B and another from point A to point C, there is a natural tendency to visualize the curves as follows:

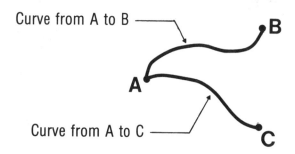

Figure 7-9

The curves as shown have only point A in common, but the second curve drawn (from A) could follow the first curve, as far as was desired, before reaching point C. Observe Figure 7-10.

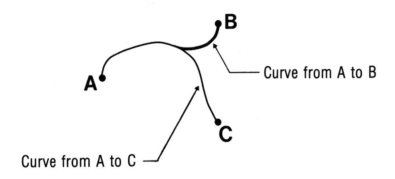

Figure 7-10

This simple "overlapping of paths" technique can be used to create unexpected shapes or to improve the appearance of expected shapes, as we observed in some of Escher's drawings and in the last example of the football player.

Improving the parallelogram dog-shape shown earlier on page 52, consider parallelogram ABCD with top and bottom curves from A to B and C to D (as shown in Figure 7-11).

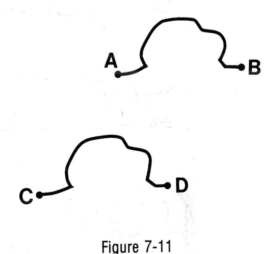

Figure 7-11

When drawing the side curve from B to D, notice the overlap along part of the top curve near B (Figure 7-12).

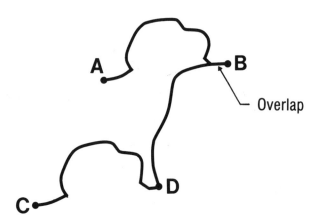

Figure 7-12

Drawing the same curve from A to C as was drawn from B to D completes the region, and the dog looks like this:

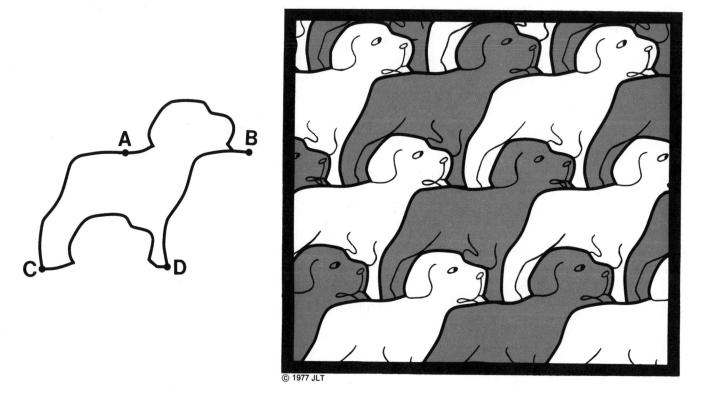

© 1977 JLT

Figure 7-13

Escher's drawing of fish and ships might be analyzed as having a parallelogram as its basis.

M. C. Escher. Untitled Work

Figure 7-14

The opposite sides are altered by translation. *Notice that the alterations overlap.*

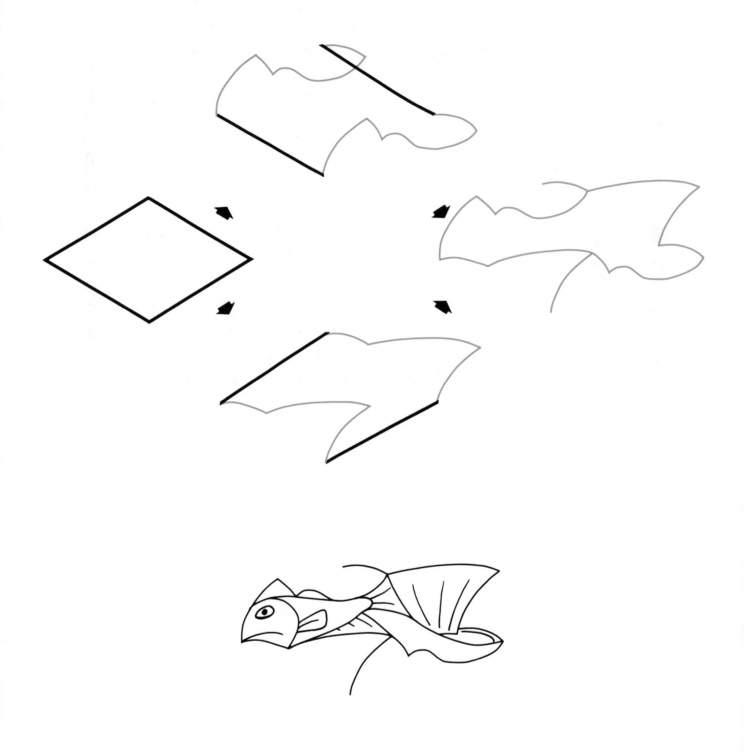

Figure 7-15

Another technique that might be used for analyzing or creating a drawing is shown in Figure 7-16. Suppose that instead of Figure 7-15 being used as the basis for the drawing, Figure 7-16 were used. The basis would then be rectangle ABCD.

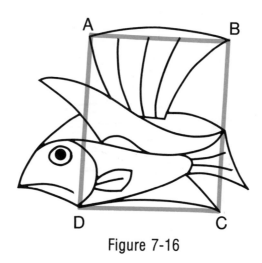

Figure 7-16

It is apparent that the alteration of $\overline{AB}$ has been translated to $\overline{DC}$ (Figure 7-17).

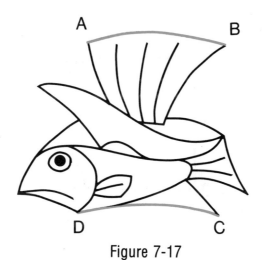

Figure 7-17

147

However, the alteration of $\overline{AD}$ can not be made to coincide with the alteration of $\overline{BC}$ by translation, rotation, reflection, or any combination of those transformations.

Figure 7-18

On the other hand, the rectangle ABCD could be thought of as a hexagon (Figure 7-19).

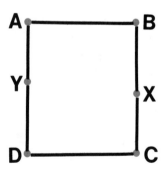

Figure 7-19

In hexagon ABXCDY, opposite sides are $\overline{AB}$ and $\overline{DC}$, $\overline{BX}$ and $\overline{YD}$, $\overline{XC}$ and $\overline{AY}$. Figure 7-20 shows the rectangle as a hexagon whose parallel, congruent opposite sides have been altered by translation.

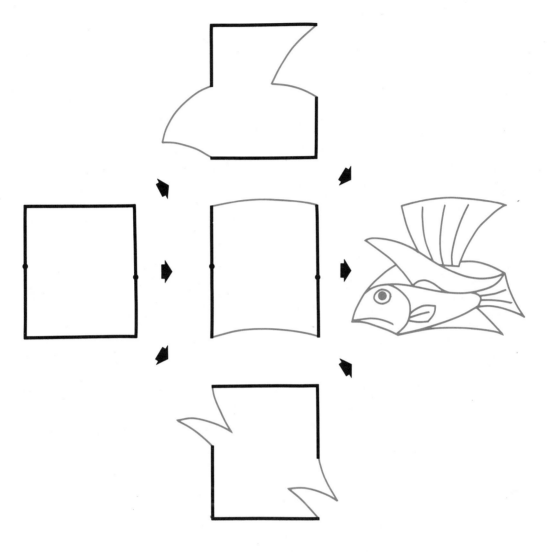

Figure 7-20

This new technique of dividing a parallelogram into a hexagon whose opposite sides are parallel and congruent may be helpful to you for creating shapes without having to visualize overlapping alterations.

Creating Escher-type drawings requires involvement through active participation. Practice, trial and error, and self discovery will make your creations more rewarding. Chapter 8 contains 18 worksheets that will help provide practice in the fundamental techniques of creating animated tessellations. Chapter 9 contains a number of selected grids which can be used beneath tracing paper as the basis for creating your patterns. Enjoy yourself!

WORKSHEETS FOR DEVELOPING TECHNIQUES

CHAPTER
EIGHT

Sketch, trace, or construct a translation of the curve to the opposite side of the parallelogram. The area of the new figure should be the same as the original parallelogram.

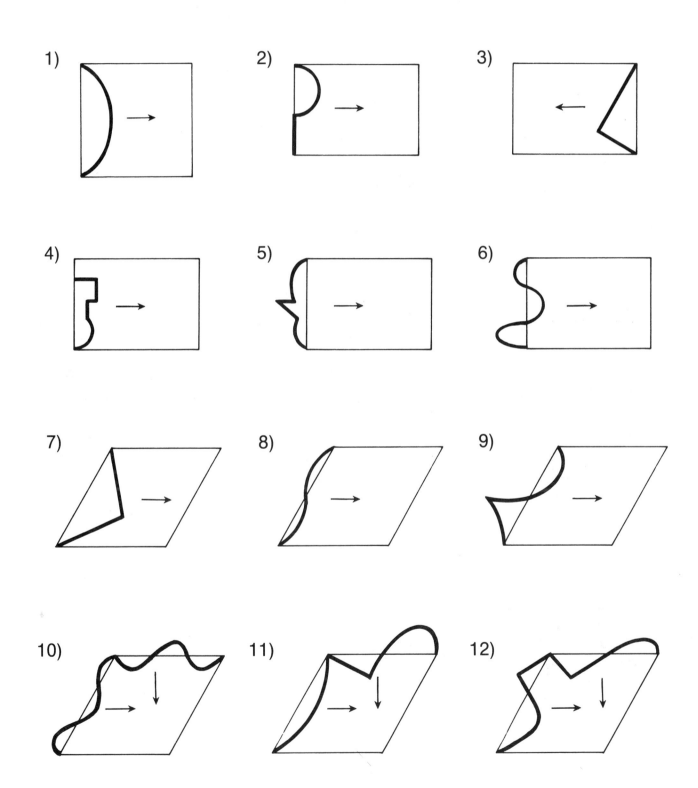

Sketch, trace, or construct a rotation of the curve about its endpoint to the adjacent side. The area of the new figure should remain the same as the area of the original figure.

1)
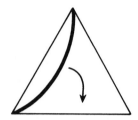

2)

3)

4)
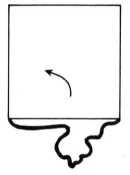

5)
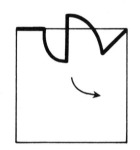

6)
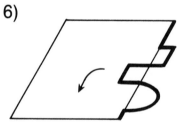

7)
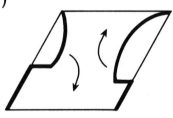

8)

9)

REFLECTION

Sketch, trace, or construct a reflection of the given curve about the given line of symmetry.

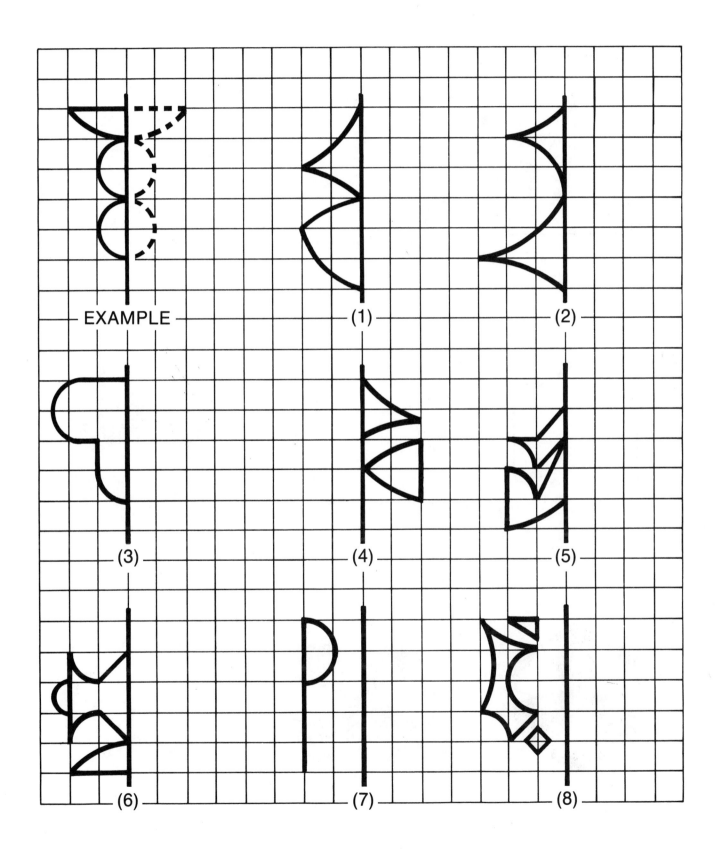

EXAMPLE (1) (2)

(3) (4) (5)

(6) (7) (8)

Draw in all the lines of symmetry in each figure below. (Some figures may not have any lines of symmetry.)

EXAMPLE

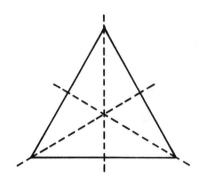

1)

2)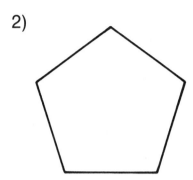

3)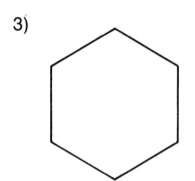

4)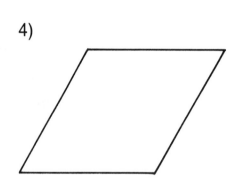

5)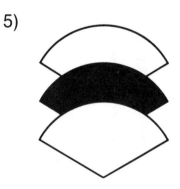

6)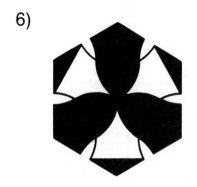

7)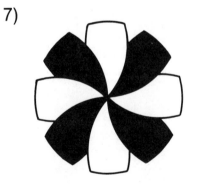

8)

The example below shows a method of creating a figure (△A'B'C') that has point symmetry with a given figure (△ABC) about a given point (P).

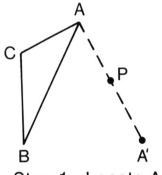

Step 1: Locate A'

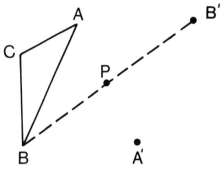

Step 2: Locate B'

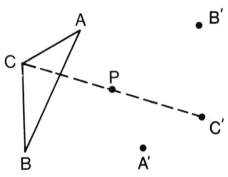

Step 3: Locate C'

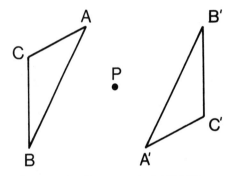

Step 4: Draw △A'B'C'

Locate a triangle that has point symmetry with △DEF about point P.

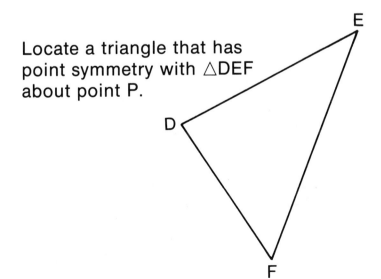

POINT SYMMETRY CONSTRUCTIONS

Sketch, trace, or construct figures that have point symmetry around point P.

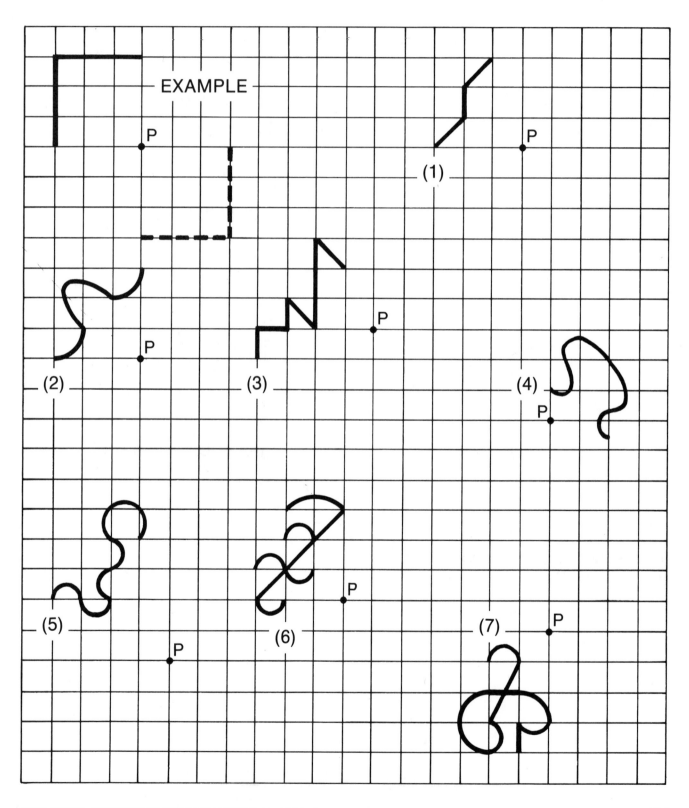

## TESSELLATION BY TRANSLATION    

Sketch, trace, or construct the translation of the curve or curves to the opposite side(s) to create a tessellating shape. Use the grid to demonstrate that the shape tessellates.

### EXAMPLE

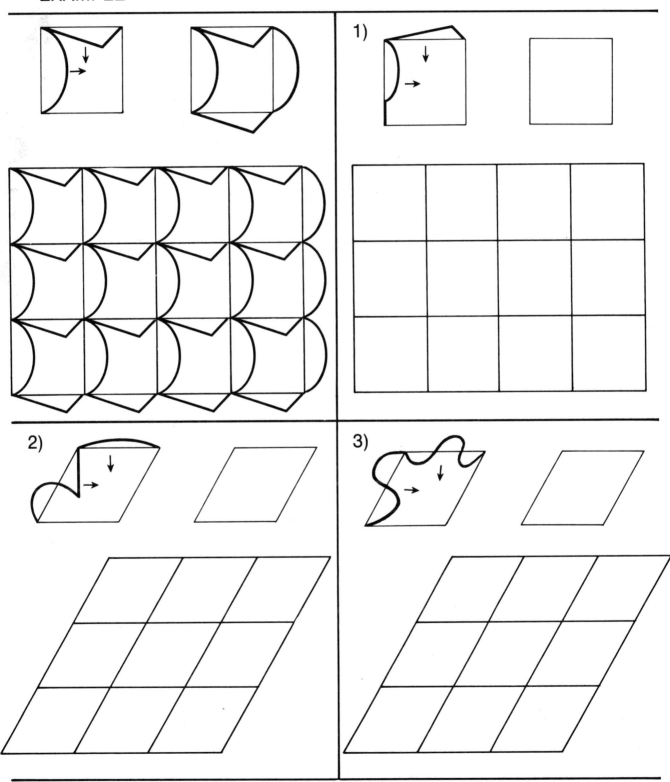

1)

2)

3)

1) Alter one side of the basic cell on the left. 2) Translate the altered side to the opposite side of the cell. 3) Use the grid to show that the shape tessellates.

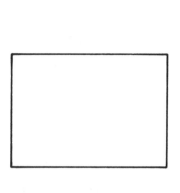

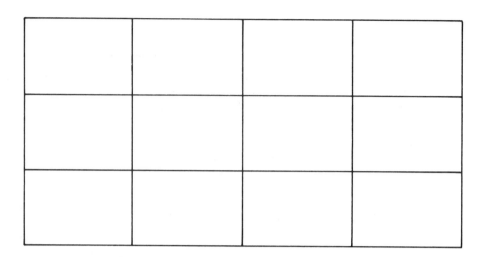

4) Alter two adjacent sides of the parallelogram. 5) Translate the altered sides to the opposite sides of the cell. 6) Use the grid to show that the shape tessellates.

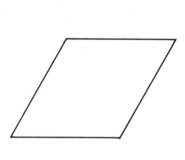

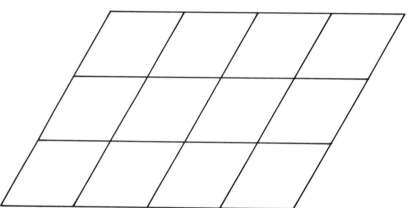

7) Alter sides AB, BC, and CD. 8) Translate the alterations to their opposite sides. 9) Use the grid to show that the shape tessellates.

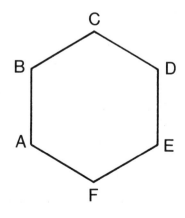

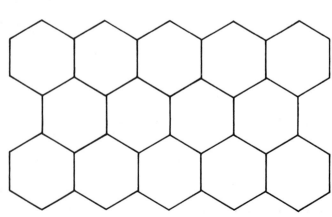

Sketch, trace, or construct the rotation of the curve as indicated. Then use the grid to demonstrate that the shape tessellates.

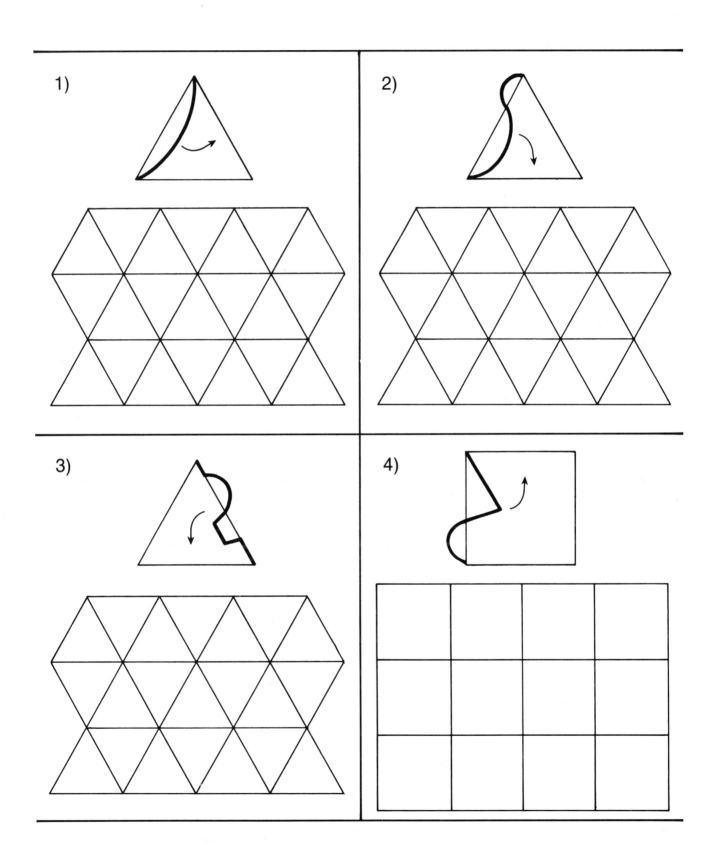

Sketch, trace, or construct the rotation of the curve or curves as indicated. Then use the grid to demonstrate that the shape tessellates.

1)

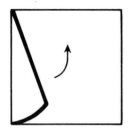

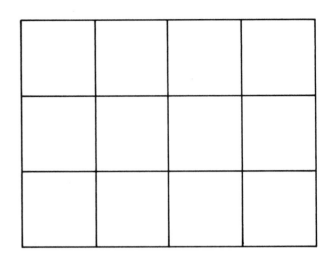

2)

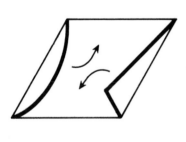

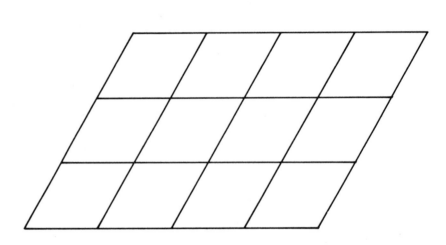

3)

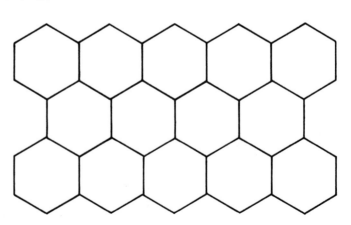

Sketch, trace, or construct the rotation of the curve about the midpoint of each segment below.

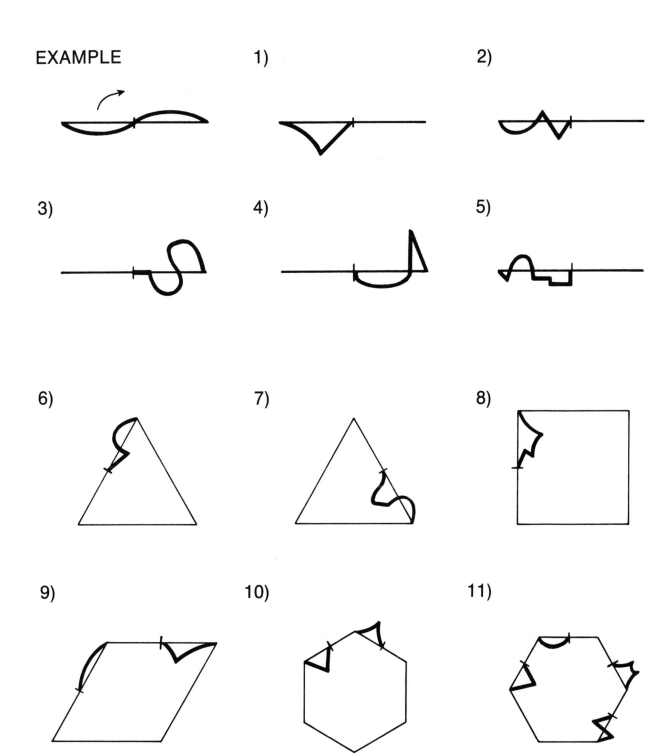

EXAMPLE

1)

2)

3)

4)

5)

6)

7)

8)

9)

10)

11)

In each example below, sketch, trace, or construct the rotation of curve AB about point B to side CB. Then trace or construct the rotation of curve AP about point P to side CP.

EXAMPLE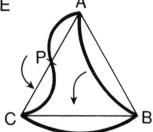

1)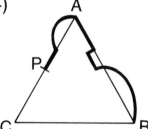

2)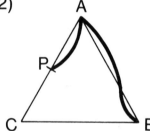

3)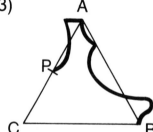

4)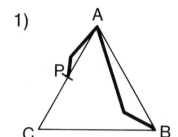

5)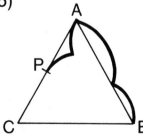

6)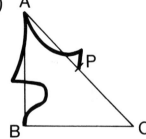

7)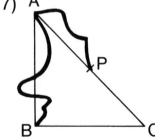

Each triangle below has been altered by rotations. Show that each shape tessellates.

Do your work on tracing paper and tape it to the worksheet.

1)

2)

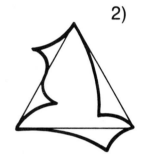

3)

4)

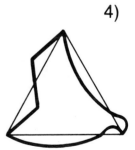

Sketch, trace, or construct the reflection of the curve about the altitude of the triangle.

EXAMPLE

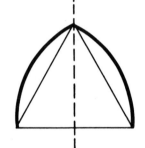

1)

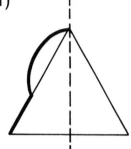

2)

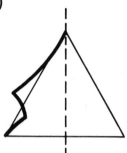

3)

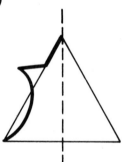

4)

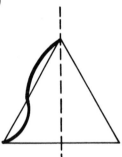

5)

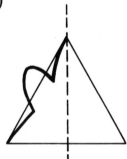

6)

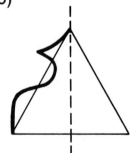

7)

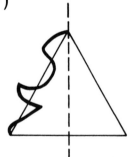

8)

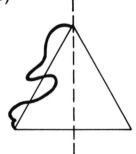

REFLECTIONS AND ROTATIONS

In step 1, trace the reflection of the given curve. In step 2, draw the rotation of the reflection about the midpoint of the line.

EXAMPLE

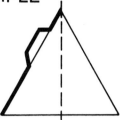
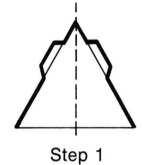
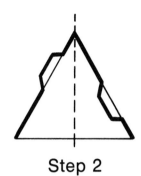

Step 1          Step 2

1)

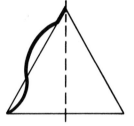
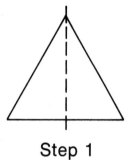
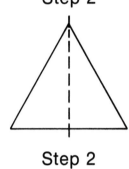

Step 1          Step 2

2)

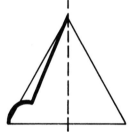
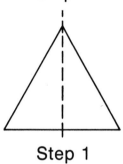
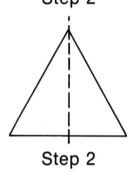

Step 1          Step 2

3)

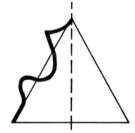
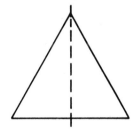
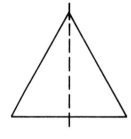

Step 1          Step 2

4)

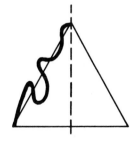
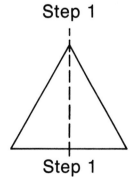
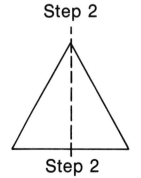

Step 1          Step 2

In each of the figures below, one side of the original triangle has been altered, then rotated about its endpoint to a second side. The third side has been changed by rotating an alteration about its midpoint. Show that these shapes tessellate.

---

1)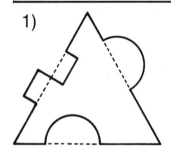

2)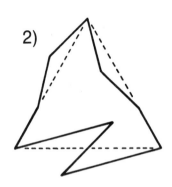

3)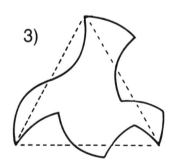

In each of the figures below, one side of the original triangle has been 1) altered, 2) reflected to another side, and finally, 3) rotated about the midpoint of that side. The third side has been changed by rotating an alteration about its midpoint. Show that these shapes tessellate.

1)

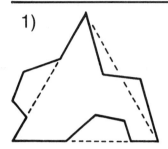

2)

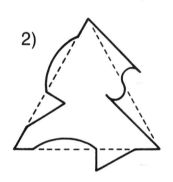

3)

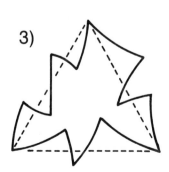

Both shapes below tessellate. Imagine each shape to be a person, an animal, or an object of some kind. Fill in the art work as you like, and create a tessellation.

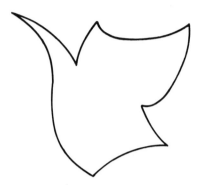

SELECTED GRIDS

CHAPTER NINE

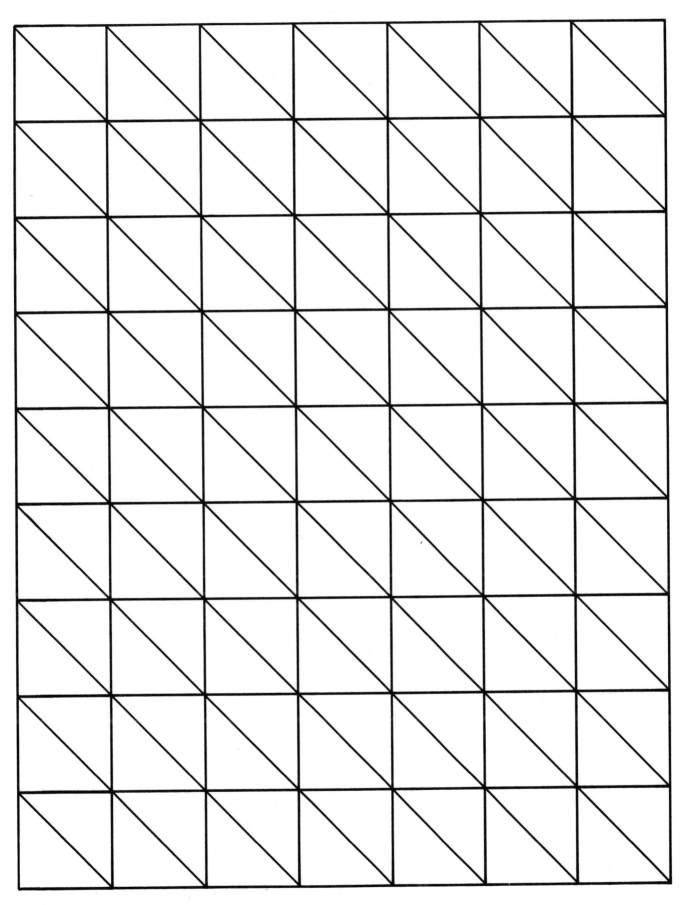

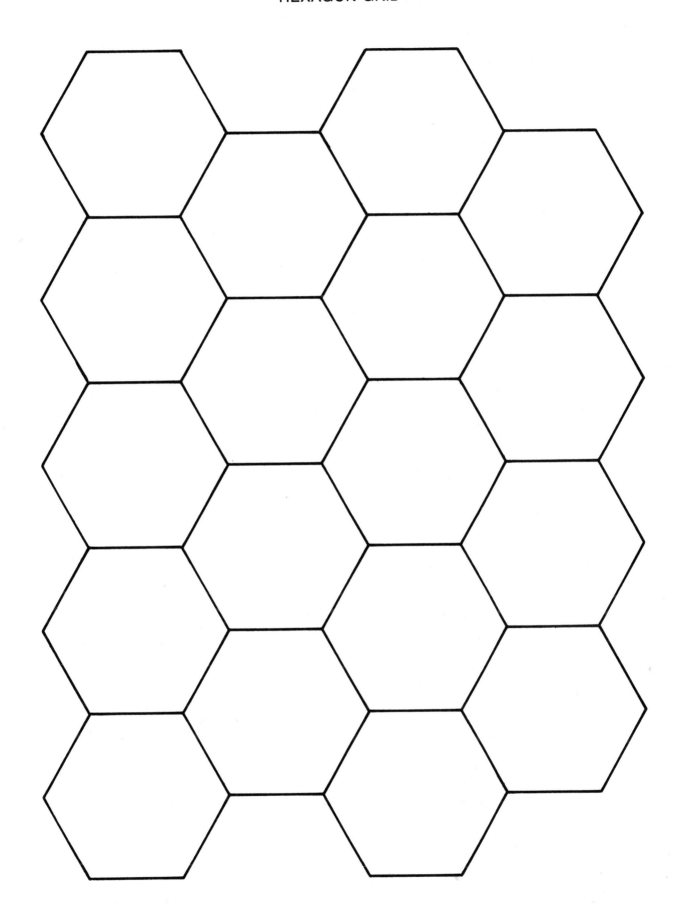

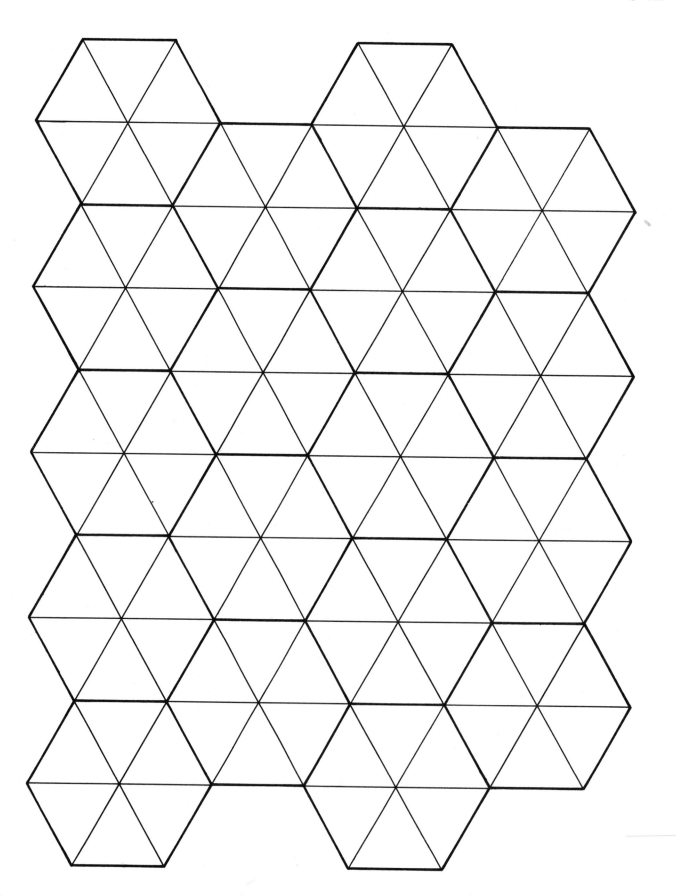

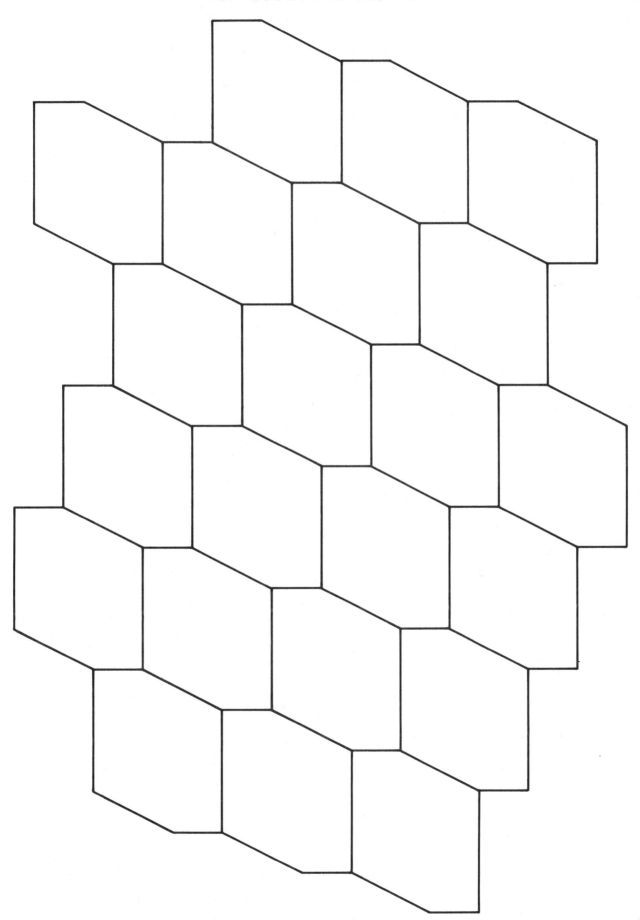

# BIBLIOGRAPHY

Bezuszka, S., Kenney, M., and Silvey, L. *Tessellations: The Geometry of Patterns.* Palo Alto, CA: Creative Publications, Inc., 1977.

Bolster, L. Carey. "Tessellations." *The Mathematics Teacher,* Vol. 66, No. 4 (April 1973), pp. 339–342.

Critchlow, Keith. *Islamic Patterns.* London: Thames and Hudson, 1976.

El-Said, Issam, and Parman, Ayse. *Geometric Concepts in Islamic Art.* London: World of Islam Festival Publishing, Ltd., 1976.

Ernst, Bruno. *The Magic Mirror of M.C. Escher,* trans. John E. Brigham. New York: Random House, 1976.

Escher, M.C. *The Graphic Work of M.C. Escher.* New York: Ballantine Books, 1967.

Gardner, Martin. "The Art of M.C. Escher," *Mathematical Carnival.* New York: Vintage Books, 1977.

Haak, Sheila. "Transformation Geometry and the Artwork of M.C. Escher." *The Mathematics Teacher,* Vol. 69, No. 8 (December 1976), pp. 647–652.

Locher, J.L., ed. *The World of M.C. Escher.* New York: Harry N. Abrams, Inc. Publishers, 1971.

Mac Gillavry, Caroline H. *Symmetry Aspects of M.C. Escher's Periodic Drawings.* Utrecht: A. Oosthoek's Uitgeversmaatschappij NV, published for the International Union of Crystallography, 1965.

Maletsky, Evan M. "Designs with Tessellations." *The Mathematics Teacher,* Vol. 67, No. 4 (April 1974), pp. 335–338.

O'Daffer, Phares G., and Clemens, Stanley R. *Geometry: An Investigative Approach.* Menlo Park, CA: Addison-Wesley Publishing Co., 1976.

————. *Laboratory Investigations in Geometry.* Menlo Park, CA: Addison-Wesley Publishing Co., 1976.

Ranucci, Ernest R. "Master of Tessellations: M.C. Escher, 1898–1972." *The Mathematics Teacher,* Vol. 67, No. 4 (April 1974), pp. 229–306.

————. "Space Filling in Two Dimensions." *The Mathematics Teacher,* Vol. 64, No. 7 (November 1971), pp. 587–593.

————. "Tiny Treasury of Tessellations." *The Mathematics Teacher,* Vol. 61, No. 2 (February 1968), pp. 114–117.

Shubnikov, A.V. *Symmetry in Science and Art,* trans. David Harker. New York and London: Plenum Press, 1974.

Teeters, Joseph L. "How to Draw Tessellations of the Escher Type." *The Mathematics Teacher,* Vol. 67, No. 4 (April 1974), pp. 307–310.

## ESCHER'S LIFE AND ART

Maurits Cornelis Escher, a Dutch artist, was born in the Netherlands at Leeuwarden on June 17, 1898. His early training in art was traditional. Escher studied for two years with a Portuguese artist, Samuel Jessurun de Mesquita, at the School of Architecture and Ornamental Design in Haarlem. Under Mesquita's tutelage, Escher mastered the graphic techniques of woodcut, wood engraving, and lithograph.

Escher migrated to Italy in 1922, settled in Rome, and remained there until 1935. While in Italy, he married and had a family. He traveled extensively throughout southern Italy, alone or in the company of other artists, observing and sketching the landscapes and buildings. He then made woodcuts from the sketches and impressions that he brought back home with him.

Figure A-1 is typical of Escher's work up until 1935. There is little in his landscape prints, other than an apparent concern with spatial structure, to suggest the Escher who was to come, the Escher of repetitive patterns and tessellating drawings. Present, however, is the expertise of the master craftsman, the obvious command of his favorite medium —the woodcut.

Later Escher lived in Switzerland, then in Belgium. He finally settled in Baarn, the Netherlands, in 1941, and spent most of the rest of his life there until his death in 1972.

The Escher most people know, the artist preoccupied with space filling of a repetitive nature, developed from an interest in the work of Moorish artists. (The Moors occupied Spain from 711 to 1492.) In 1936, while traveling through southern Spain, Escher visited the Alhambra in Granada.

Figure A-1

M. C. Escher. *Coast of Amalfi.* Woodcut, 1934

He studied intently the Moorish mosaics on the walls and floors of the Alhambra. He copied the motifs of the tiles in his notebook, and used them later in his prints. The mosaics fascinated him and renewed the curiosity that had prompted him to some experimentation with tessellating drawings as early as 1922 and 1926.

Though inspired by the Moorish tiles, Escher preferred recognizable, animate figures to purely geometric patterns in his drawings. He commented (Escher, 1971):

> This is the richest source of inspiration that I have ever struck; nor has it yet dried up. The symmetry drawings . . . show how a surface can be regularly divided into, or filled up with, similar-shaped figures which are contiguous to one another, without leaving any open spaces. The Moors were past masters of this. They decorated walls and floors, particularly in the Alhambra in Spain, by placing congruent, multi-coloured pieces of majolica together without leaving any spaces between. What a pity it is that Islam did not permit them to make "graven images." They always restricted themselves, in their massed tiles, to designs of an abstract geometrical type. Not one single Moorish artist, to the best of my knowledge, ever made so bold (or maybe the idea never occurred to him) as to use concrete, recognisable, naturistically conceived figures of fish, birds, reptiles or human beings as elements in their surface coverage. This restriction is all the more unacceptable to me in that the recognizability of the components of my own designs is the reason for my unfailing interest in this sphere.

Escher so enjoyed the tessellating animate figures that he said (Mac Gillavry, 1965):

> The dynamic action of making a symmetric tessellation is done more or less unconsciously. While drawing I sometimes feel as if I were a spiritualist medium, controlled by the creatures which I am conjuring up. It is as if they themselves decide on the shape in which they choose to appear. They take little account of my critical opinion during their birth and I cannot exert much influence on the measure of their development. They usually are very difficult and obstinate creatures.

Escher's style of art changed dramatically after 1937. Not only did his visit to the Alhambra influence him, but also his change of location. Prior to his move from Italy, he had illustrated landscapes and architecture. When he found the landscapes and architecture of Switzerland, Belgium, and Holland less striking than that of southern Italy, he began to concentrate more on communicating his own personal ideas and explorations through his art. Figures A-2 and A-3 are examples of Escher's art after 1937.

Figure A-2

M. C. Escher. *Concave and Convex.* Lithograph, 1955

Figure A-3

M. C. Escher. Untitled Work

It is a curious fact that Escher's prints should be so inextricably tied up with mathematics; he was no trained mathematician. Escher himself expressed surprise at this fact when he said of some of his work (Escher, 1971):

> . . . The ideas that are basic to them often bear witness to my amazement and wonder at the laws of nature which operate in the world around us. He who wonders discovers that this is in itself a wonder. By keenly confronting the enigmas that surround us, and by considering and analyzing the observations that I had made, I ended up in the domain of mathematics. Although I am absolutely without training or knowledge in the exact sciences, I often seem to have more in common with mathematicians than with my fellow artists.

Escher was likewise surprised to learn that some of the basic rules of periodic space-filling, which he had so arduously worked to discover and communicate, had already been discovered by the science of crystallography. It is interesting to note Escher's response to an illustrated article on the seventeen crystalline forms, written by Dr. George Polya and published in 1924 by *Geitshrift für Kristallographic*, a European scientific journal. According to Dr. Polya, Professor Emeritus of Stanford University and recognized authority on problem-solving techniques, he received a letter from Escher regarding the article and including samples of Escher's work.

Crystal formations, like the Moorish mosaics, became another rich source from which Escher drew material for his drawings. Many of his works were based on the principles of crystallography and color symmetry. Escher, who made his own first tessellating woodcut in 1922—a collection of eight different human heads—found in the Moorish approach and in crystallography the keys to much of his life's work. He simply adapted Moorish solutions and nature's solutions, with a prodigious inventiveness of his own.

For many years, when his art was neither understood nor respected by art critics and his colleagues, Escher continued to explore and communicate his findings through his art. Today, Escher's work is not only well-known and popular with the buying public, but is also highly respected by artists, mathematicians, and scientists.

*References*

Ernst, Bruno. *The Magic Mirror of M.C. Escher,* trans. John E. Brigham. New York: Random House, First American Edition, 1976.

Escher, M.C. *The Graphic Work of M.C. Escher,* trans. John E. Brigham. New York: Ballantine Books, 1971.

Locher, J.L., ed. *The World of M.C. Escher.* New York: Harry N. Abrams, Inc. Publishers, 1971.

Mac Gillavry, Caroline H. *Symmetry Aspects of M.C. Escher's Periodic Drawings.* Utrecht: A. Oosthoek's Uitgeversmaatschappij NV, published for the International Union of Crystallography, 1965.

Polya, George. Personal interview, Palo Alto, California, 1977.

Ranucci, Ernest R. "Master of Tessellations: M.C. Escher, 1898–1972." *The Mathematics Teacher,* Vol. 67, No. 4 (April 1974), pp. 300–306.

CREATIVE PUBLICATIONS MATH DESIGN SERIES
*Creating Escher-type Drawings* by Ranucci and Teeters
*Creative Constructions* by Seymour and Schadler
*Designs from Mathematical Patterns* by Bezuszka, Kenney, and Silvey
*Geo-Ring Polyhedra* by Silvey
*Kaleidoscope Math* by Kennedy and Thomas
*Line Designs* by Seymour, Silvey, and Snider
*Paper and Scissors Polygons* by Silvey and Taylor
*Pattern Blocks Coloring Book* by Silvey and Pasternack
*Patterns in Space* by Beard
*Seeing Shapes* by Ranucci
*Straw Polyhedra* by Laycock
*String Sculpture* by Winter
*Tessellations: The Geometry of Pattern* by Bezuszka, Kenney, and Silvey